TUNE IN 1

Student Book

Learning English Through Listening

Jack C. Richards
& Kerry O'Sullivan

OXFORD
UNIVERSITY PRESS

OXFORD
UNIVERSITY PRESS

198 Madison Avenue
New York, NY 10016 USA

Great Clarendon Street, Oxford OX2 6DP UK

Oxford University Press is a department of the University of Oxford.
It furthers the University's objective of excellence in research, scholarship,
and education by publishing worldwide in

Oxford   New York

Auckland   Cape Town   Dar es Salaam   Hong Kong   Karachi
Kuala Lumpur   Madrid   Melbourne   Mexico City   Nairobi
New Delhi   Shanghai   Taipei   Toronto

With offices in

Argentina   Austria   Brazil   Chile   Czech Republic   France   Greece
Guatemala   Hungary   Italy   Japan   Poland   Portugal   Singapore
South Korea   Switzerland   Thailand   Turkey   Ukraine   Vietnam

OXFORD and OXFORD ENGLISH are registered trademarks of
Oxford University Press

© Oxford University Press 2006

Database right Oxford University Press (maker)

Library of Congress Cataloging-in-Publication Data

Richards, Jack C.

Tune In—learning English through listening: Student book / Jack C. Richards
& Kerry O'Sullivan.

p. cm.

Includes indexes.

ISBN: 978-0-19-447101-5 (student book 1)

ISBN: 978-0-19-447100-8 (student book 1 with CD)

1. English language—Textbooks for foreign speakers. 2. Listening—Problems,
exercises, etc. I. Title: Learining English through listening. II. O'Sullivan, Kerry,
1952-. III. Title.

PE1128.R469 2006

448.3'421—dc22

2006040033

No unauthorized photocopying

Senior Acquisitions Editor: Chris Balderston
Editor: Emma Gonin
Associate Editor: Hannah Ryu
Assistant Editor: Kate Schubert
Art Director: Maj-Britt Hagsted
Senior Designer: Mia Gomez
Art Editor: Robin Fadool
Production Manager: Shanta Persaud
Production Controller: Zainaltu Jawat Ali

STUDENT BOOK ISBN: 978 0 19 447101 5
PACK ISBN: 978 0 19 447100 8
Printed in China

Printing (last digit) 10   9   8

ACKNOWLEDGMENTS:

Illustrations by: Glenn Urieta: 3, 7, 28, 50, 64, 91; Geo Parkin/AA Reps: 4, 25,
51, 69, 88; Guy Holt: 5, 22, 46, 62, 87; Harry Briggs: 10, 16, 43, 45, 49, 58, 67,
82, 89; William Waitzman: 13, 52, 81; Scott MacNeill: 14, 37; Stephen Linnell/
Three in a Box: 15, 76, 83, 90; Cybele/Three in a Box: 18, 57; Lisa Smith/Sylvie
Poggio Artists Agency: 19, 48, 79; Karen Minot: 19, 26, 72, 82; Graham White/
NB Illustration: 32, 35, 36, 37; Adrian Barclay/Beehive Illustration: 37, 73; Katie

Mac/NB Illustration: 40, 86; Jon Proctor/Shannon Associates: 34, 47, 67 85; Mona
Daly/Mendola Art: 53, 65, 70; Tony Forbes/Sylvie Poggio Artists Agency: 24, 53, 55,
61, 74; Francis Bacon/Specs Art: 68; Mark Duffin: 77

*We would like to thank the following for their permission to reproduce the photographs
on the cover and in the introduction:* Getty: Daniel Allen, (listening to music);
Punchstock: (raising hand in class); Punchstock: (whispering); Punchstock: (group
of friends jumping);; Punchstock: (talking on a cell phone); Punchstock: (holding a
CD); Punchstock: (student smiling).

We would like to thank the following for their permission to reproduce photographs:
Globe Photos Inc.: Fitzroy Barrett, 2 (Nicole Kidman); Globe Photos Inc.: Andrea
Renault, 2 (Jennifer Lopez); Starmaxinc.om: DP/AAD, 2 (Will Smith); Wireimage.
com: Jean Baptiste Lacroix, 2 (Jackie Chan); Image State: 5; Getty: Digital Vision, 6;
Image State: 8; Image State: 8; Image State: 8; Getty: Robert Warren, 8; Masterfile:
Simon DesRochers, 8; David Wootton Photography: 8 (palm pilot); Photoedit
Inc.: David Young-Wolff, 9; Photographers Direct: Danja Kohler/ Images of Africa,
11; Photographers Direct: Macana Ltd., 12; Punchstock: 14; Punchstock: 17
(karate); Art Directors & Trip Photo Library: 17 (dancing); Punchstock: 17 (eating
lunch); Punchstock: 17 (haircut); Punchstock: 17 (shopping); Picturequest: 20
(can of soda); Photographers Direct: 20 (fashion magazine); Richard B. Levine: 20
(comic book); Age Fotostock: 20 (digital camera); Photo Edit Inc.: Rudi Von Briel,
20 (t-shirts); Photoedit Inc.: Lon C. Diehl, 20 (skateboard); Punchstock: www.
imagesource.com, 20 (sandals); Photo Edit Inc.: Colin Young-Wolff, 20 (men's
jeans); Age Fotostock: Ben Welsh, 20 (camera phone); Photo Edit Inc.: Michael
Newman, 21 (basketball shoes); Photoedit Inc.: Lon C. Diehl, 21 (skateboard); The
Image Works: Topham, 21 (camera phone); Photographers Direct: 23 (fashion
magazine); Punchstock: 23 (cookie); Punchstock: 23 (baseball cap); The Image
Works: Science & Society Picture Library, 23 (digital camera); Photo Edit Inc.:
Raquel Ramirez, 23 (comics); Picturequest: 23 (golf ball); Photographers Direct:
23 (doughnut); Punchstock: 23 (shopping); Masterfile: 26; Punchstock: 27;
Classmates Media Inc.: 29 (high school picture); Associated Press: Lenny Ignelzi,
29 (Masters Tournament 1997); Getty: Andrew Redington, 29 (Tiger Woods and
Elin Nordegren); Image State: 30; Classmates Media Inc.: 31 (1990 photo with
mother); Associated Press: Reed Saxon, 31 (backstage with her best actress
Oscar); The Everett Collection: Rex Features, 31 (with baby, Apple); Starmaxinc.:
Morrison/Haller/AAD, 31 (Gwyneth Paltrow and Chris Martin); Punchstock: 32
(Lake Biwa); Elk Photography: 32 (Wat Chiang Man); Alamy: 32 (Menara Kuala
Lumpur); Photographers Direct: Louisa Forrester, 33; Robertstock: 35; Image
State: 38 (laptop); Dennis Light: 38 (bike riding); Photographers Direct: 38 (text
message); Photoedit Inc.: Dana White, 38 (reading a comic book); Photoedit
Inc.: Robert Brenner, 38 (playing volleyball); Punchstock: 38 (listening to music);
Punchstock: 39 (Sophie); Punchstock: 39 (Young-woo); Punchstock: 39 (Carl); Getty:
Stephen Simpson, 39 (Amy); Associated Press: Frank Franklin Ii, 41 (winning
dog); The Image Works: Lee Snider Photo Images, 41 (sightseeing bus); Image
State: 41 (shopping in an electronics store); Punchstock: 41 (dog with a ribbon);
Photographers Direct: Louisa Forrester, 42; Image State: 44 (playing basketball);
Robertstock: 44 (riding a skateboard); Punchstock: 44 (laptop); Igal Jusidman:
44 (purse); Punchstock: 44 (pen); Photographers Direct: Celi Azulek, 44 (men's
watch); Photographers Direct: Peter Kubal, 44 (gold bracelet); Picturequest:
46 (tv); Superstock: 46 (MP3 with digital camera); Punchstock: 46 (cell phone);
Punchstock: 46 (laptop); Ken Bannister: 47 (Banana Museum); Guinness
Book of Records: 47 (drumstick collection); John Meisenheimer: 47 (yo-yo
collection); Mia Gomez/Jason Ziemniak: 47 (colored vinyl records); Punchstock:
54; Photographers Direct: Pierre Roussel, 56 (cargo shorts); Age Fotostock: 56
(sneakers); Aurora: 56 (sweater); Frank Nowikowski: 56 (sandals); Photographers
Direct: 56 (gray flannel suit); Photographers Direct: David Withers, 56 (tie); The
Image Works: Lee Snider Photo Images, 59 (men shopping); Getty: Antonio
Mo, 59 (women shopping); Masterfile: Mark Leibowitz, 60; The Image Works:
Topham, 63 (Alicia Keys); Retna: Micky Simawi, 63 (Vanessa Mae); The Image
Works: Topham, 63 (Lang Lang); Getty: MN Chan, 66; Picturequest: 71; Photo
Edit Inc.: Bill Freeman, 75 (Jun-hao); Robertstock: 75 (Sam); Alamy: 75 (Emma);
Photographers Direct: 75 (Mei-ling); Punchstock: 75 (John); Superstock: 78; Mark
E. Gibson: 80 (leading children); The Image Works: Jim West, 80 (working in a fast
food restaurant); Age Fotostock: 80 (store cashier); The Image Works: 80 (picking
fruit); Alamy: 80 (motorcycle courier); Getty: Nicolas Russell, 80 (looking on-line);
Punchstock: 84 (Maria); Robertstock: 84 (Will); Punchstock: 84 (Sun-young);
Picturequest: 84 (Tony); Photographers Direct: Francisco Fernandez Prieto, 86.

*The publishers would like to thank the following people for their help in developing this
series:* Sookyung Chang, Korea; Tina Chen, Taiwan; June Chiang, Taiwan; Robert
Dilenschneider, Japan; Bill Hogue, Japan; Hirofumi Hosokawa, Japan; Nikko
Ying-ying Hsiang, Taiwan; Yu Young Kim, Korea; Ellen Scattergood, Japan;
Katherine Song, Korea; Damien Tresize, Taiwan; Nobuo Tsuda, Japan; I-chieh Yang,
Taiwan. *With special thanks to:* Mark Frank, Japan and Su-wei Wang, Taiwan.

The publishers would like to thank the following OUP staff for their support and assistance:
Brett Bowie, Kaoru Ito, Kerry Nockolds, and Ted Yoshioka.

Introduction

Welcome to *Tune In!* This is a three-level listening series that teaches you the two important aspects of listening: understanding *what* people say and *how* they say it. This will help you improve your English.

Student Book

There are two lessons in each of the 15 units in the Student Book. Each lesson focuses on a different aspect of the unit topic. The lessons are organized into five sections, each one with carefully graded activities. This step-by-step approach makes learning natural English much easier.

BEFORE YOU LISTEN

This section introduces the topic of the lesson and presents key vocabulary for the listening activities.

LISTEN AND UNDERSTAND

There are two **Listen and Understand** sections in each lesson that go with recordings of people talking. The activities in these sections help you understand *what* the people say. These sections help you improve your overall listening comprehension skills.

For extra practice, you can also listen to the final **Listen and Understand** of each lesson on the Student CD.

TUNE IN

This section focuses on one feature of spoken English. This helps you understand *how* people say what they want to say. This will then help you speak English in a more natural way.

AFTER YOU LISTEN

This section gives you the chance to talk to your classmates about the lesson topic. It also lets you practice the feature of spoken English from the **Tune In** section.

Audio Program

There are various types of spoken English on the CDs—from casual conversations, telephone conversations, and voice-mail messages to travel announcements, TV interviews, and radio shows. The complete audio program for the Student Book is on the Class CDs. There is also a Student CD on the inside back cover of the Student Book for self study. The Student CD contains the final **Listen and Understand** of each lesson. The track list for the Student CD is on page 92.

Scope and Sequence

Unit	Lesson	Lesson Objectives		Listening Genres
		Listen and Understand	**Tune In**	
1 Meeting People *Page 2*	1 Nice to meet you	▸ Understanding introductions ▸ Spelling people's names	Starting conversations	▸ Party conversations ▸ Casual introductions
	2 See you later	▸ Recognizing greetings and good-byes ▸ Identifying topics of conversation	Keeping conversations going	▸ Casual conversations
2 Communicating *Page 8*	1 What's your e-mail address?	▸ Recognizing numbers ▸ Spelling e-mail addresses	Asking for clarification	▸ Customer service conversations ▸ Casual conversations
	2 May I speak to Tony, please?	▸ Recognizing ways of using the telephone ▸ Identifying people's purposes	Using rising and falling intonation	▸ Telephone conversations ▸ Voice-mail messages
3 Telling Time *Page 14*	1 What time do you get up?	▸ Identifying time of day ▸ Understanding work routines	Confirming or correcting information	▸ Travel announcements & casual conversations ▸ Class conversations
	2 Are you free on Friday night?	▸ Understanding schedules ▸ Recognizing appointments	Giving polite negative answers	▸ Telephone conversations ▸ Voice-mail messages
4 Shopping *Page 20*	1 How much does it cost?	▸ Identifying prices ▸ Identifying items in a store	Using the contraction of *did you*	▸ Casual conversations ▸ Conversations with store clerks
	2 It's just what I need!	▸ Identifying stores ▸ Identifying locations in a store	Making and responding to suggestions	▸ Casual conversations ▸ Store announcements
5 Dates & Events *Page 26*	1 When's your birthday?	▸ Understanding people's plans ▸ Understanding descriptions of events	Showing interest	▸ Casual conversations
	2 So when was that?	▸ Recognizing dates ▸ Understanding descriptions of events	Using intonation in questions	▸ TV quiz show ▸ Magazine interviews
6 Places *Page 32*	1 It sounds like an interesting place	▸ Understanding descriptions of places ▸ Distinguishing facts and opinions	Expressing agreement	▸ Tour guide conversations ▸ Casual conversations
	2 How do I get there?	▸ Identifying locations ▸ Understanding directions	Checking understanding	▸ Conversations in the street ▸ Conversations at a tourist information office
7 Lifestyles *Page 38*	1 Do you ride every day?	▸ Understanding activities and routines ▸ Recognizing likes and dislikes	Using double questions	▸ Casual conversations ▸ Magazine interviews
	2 What are you going to do this weekend?	▸ Understanding descriptions of plans ▸ Identifying descriptions of events	Using the contraction of *going to*	▸ Office conversations ▸ Casual conversations
8 Possessions *Page 44*	1 Hey, that's cool!	▸ Understanding descriptions of items ▸ Recognizing features of items	Expressing enthusiasm	▸ Casual conversations ▸ Conversations with sales clerks
	2 What a terrific collection!	▸ Understanding descriptions of interests ▸ Recognizing requests	Checking understanding	▸ Radio show ▸ Telephone inquiries

Unit	Lesson	Lesson Objectives		Listening Genres
		Listen and Understand	Tune In	
9 The Body *Page 50*	1 Where does it hurt?	▶ Identifying parts of the body ▶ Recognizing descriptions of problems	Clarifying information	▶ Conversations with a doctor ▶ Telephone inquiries
	2 Now try this!	▶ Understanding instructions ▶ Understanding descriptions of exercises	Giving supporting and contrasting information	▶ Exercise class ▶ Casual conversations
10 Clothes & Fashion *Page 56*	1 I like your shirt!	▶ Identifying clothes ▶ Recognizing preferences	Expressing uncertainty	▶ Casual conversations ▶ TV interviews
	2 Where did you buy those jeans?	▶ Identifying features of clothes ▶ Understanding information about people	Expressing agreement or disagreement	▶ Casual conversations
11 Music *Page 62*	1 He's a great drummer!	▶ Recognizing descriptions of instruments ▶ Identifying information about people	Showing you are listening	▶ Conversations with a store clerk ▶ Radio show
	2 How was the concert?	▶ Understanding information about events ▶ Recognizing people's intentions	Accepting and declining invitations	▶ Radio show ▶ Casual conversations
12 Food *Page 68*	1 Would you care for a snack?	▶ Understanding offers and replies ▶ Identifying descriptions of meals	Using short forms of questions	▶ Casual conversations
	2 What are we having for dinner?	▶ Understanding recipes ▶ Understanding food orders	Checking understanding	▶ TV cooking show ▶ Telephone food orders
13 Housing *Page 74*	1 Where do you live?	▶ Understanding housing preferences ▶ Recognizing likes and dislikes	Expressing uncertainty	▶ Casual conversations ▶ Conversations with a college counselor
	2 How do you like my room?	▶ Understanding ideas and wishes ▶ Identifying changes and suggestions	Making and responding to suggestions	▶ Casual conversations ▶ Conversations with an interior designer
14 Jobs *Page 80*	1 Are you interested in sales work?	▶ Understanding and comparing abilities ▶ Understanding descriptions of jobs	Expressing agreement	▶ Casual conversations
	2 What's the job like?	▶ Understanding descriptions of job routines ▶ Recognizing descriptions of occupations	Giving supporting and contrasting information	▶ Party conversations ▶ Casual conversations
15 Talents & Abilities *Page 86*	1 Can you dance the tango?	▶ Understanding descriptions of abilities ▶ Recognizing Items from descriptions	Answering questions	▶ Casual conversations ▶ Conversations with store clerks
	2 What are you good at?	▶ Recognizing descriptions of talents ▶ Understanding information about people	Keeping conversations going	▶ Casual conversations ▶ TV talk show
Student CD Track List *Page 92*				

Meeting People

Lesson 1 Nice to meet you

1 **BEFORE YOU LISTEN**

A. Are these first names or last names? Write *first* or *last* next to each name. The first two are done for you. Then compare your answers with a partner.

1. Brown   <u>last</u>   6. Woods   _____
2. Jackie   <u>first</u>   7. Jennifer _____
3. Rowling _____   8. Kennedy _____
4. Nicole   _____   9. Will   _____
5. Peter   _____   10. Emma   _____

B. Who are these famous people? Their first names are in the list in part A. Write the first name under each photo. Then compare your answers with a partner.

1. _____ Kidman   2. _____ Lopez   3. _____ Smith   4. _____ Chan

2 **LISTEN AND UNDERSTAND** CD 1 Track 02

A. People are introducing themselves at a party. What are their first names? Listen and number these names from 1 to 6. The first one is done for you.

a. Sumio ____   c. David ____   e. Sarah ____
b. John _1_   d. Matt ____   f. Hannah ____

B. Listen again. Check (✓) the expression you hear in each conversation. The first one is done for you.

1. a. Nice to see you. ____   b. Nice to meet you. _✓_
2. a. Good to meet you anyway. ____   b. Good to meet you, by the way. ____
3. a. Anyway, my name's Sarah. ____   b. By the way, my name's Sarah. ____
4. a. What's your name again? ____   b. Who are you again? ____
5. a. Do you mean me? ____   b. Remember me?____
6. a. Sorry, is it Anna? ____   b. Sorry, did you say Anna? ____

3 LISTEN AND UNDERSTAND 🎧 CD 1 Tracks 03 & 04

A. People are putting each other's names in their cell phones. Listen and finish the spelling of each name. The first one is done for you.

1. M a r i e
2. S __ __ - j i
3. S __ __ __ n

4. __ a z __
5. P __ __ t __ __
6. __ __ __ __ i a n

B. Listen to the rest of the conversations. Write the other person's name in each conversation. The first one is done for you.

1. Y u - t i n g
2. __ __ __ __ __ __ __
3. __ __ __ __ __

4. __ __ __ __ __ __ __ __
5. __ __ __ __ __
6. __ __ - __ __ __ __ __ __

4 TUNE IN 🎧 CD 1 Tracks 05 & 06

A. Listen and notice how people start conversations at a party by talking about the party, the music, and the food.

A: *Nice party, isn't it?*	A: *Great music, isn't it?*	A: *Are you enjoying the food?*
B: *Yeah, it's great.*	B: *Yeah, it is.*	B: *Yes, I am.*

B. Now listen to other people at a party. What does the person talk about to start each conversation? Number these topics from 1 to 4.

a. the music ___

b. the guests ___

c. the weather ___

d. the food ___

AFTER YOU LISTEN

A. Choose the correct question in the box to complete each conversation. Then practice the conversations with a partner.

> Are you enjoying the food?
> Do you know everybody here?
> Great music, isn't it?

1. A: _____?
   B: *Yeah, it's perfect for dancing.*
   A: *This is my favorite band.*
   B: *Mine, too.*

2. A: _____?
   B: *Yes, it's delicious.*
   A: *Have you tried these?*
   B: *Not yet. They look good.*

3. A: _____?
   B: *No, not really.*
   A: *Come and meet some of my friends.*
   B: *Thanks. I'd love to.*

B. Match each expression with its response. The first one is done for you. Then practice the conversations with a partner.

1. Nice to meet you. __e__   **a.** Hi, Yvonne. I'm Naoko.
2. How are you? ___   **b.** No, I'm Andrew.
3. By the way, are you Peter? ___   **c.** Pretty good, thanks.
4. We haven't met. I'm Yvonne. ___   **d.** It's Jennifer.
5. What's your name again? ___   **e.** Nice to meet you, too.

C. Role-play. You are at a party. Talk to three other guests using this conversation. Replace the highlighted parts with expressions in the boxes and your own information.

> Nice party, isn't it?   Beautiful weather, isn't it?   Great food, isn't it?

> great   nice   fantastic

> By the way, my name's. . .   Anyway, I'm. . .

> Good to meet you.   Nice to meet you.   Great to meet you.

A: *Hi! Great music, isn't it?*
B: *Yeah, it's wonderful. Hey, my name's Akio.*
A: *Nice to meet you. I'm Sophie.*
B: *Good to meet you. How are you?*
A: *Pretty good, thanks. And you?*
B: *Fine, thanks.*

LESSON OBJECTIVES
▸ Recognizing greetings and good-byes
▸ Identifying topics of conversation
▸ Keeping conversations going

Lesson 2 See you later

1 BEFORE YOU LISTEN

Do you use these expressions when you greet people or when you say good-bye?
Check (✓) the correct column. The first one is done for you. Then compare your answers
with a partner.

	Greeting people	Saying good-bye
1. Have a nice day.	☐	☑
2. See you later.	☐	☐
3. How are things?	☐	☐
4. How's it going?	☐	☐
5. What's up?	☐	☐
6. Talk to you later.	☐	☐
7. How is everything?	☐	☐
8. Bye for now.	☐	☐
9. Catch you later.	☐	☐
10. How have you been?	☐	☐

2 LISTEN AND UNDERSTAND 🎧 CD 1 Track 07

A. People are talking to their friends. Are they greeting their friends or saying good-bye?
Listen and check (✓) the correct column.

	Greeting people	Saying good-bye
1.	☐	☐
2.	☐	☐
3.	☐	☐
4.	☐	☐
5.	☐	☐
6.	☐	☐

B. Listen again. Where are the people talking? Number these pictures from 1 to 6.

a. a supermarket ___   c. a movie theater ___   e. a cafe ___

b. a beach ___   d. a department store ___   f. a bus stop ___

③ LISTEN AND UNDERSTAND 🎧 CD 1 Track 08

A. People are greeting their friends. What do they talk about after they greet each other? Listen and circle the correct topic. The first one is done for you.

1. **a.** the weather **b.** music
2. **a.** food **b.** clothes
3. **a.** school **b.** work
4. **a.** studying **b.** shopping
5. **a.** movies **b.** vacation

B. Listen again. Do both people have the same plans? Check (✓) the correct column.

	Same	Different
1.	☐	☐
2.	☐	☐
3.	☐	☐
4.	☐	☐
5.	☐	☐

④ TUNE IN 🎧 CD 1 Tracks 09 & 10

A. Listen and notice how people keep conversations going by asking follow-up questions.

> **A:** *It's really hot today, isn't it?*
> **B:** *Yeah. I'm going to the pool.* ***How about you?***
>
> **A:** *How's your job going?*
> **B:** *Pretty good, but I'm really busy this month.* ***What about you?***
>
> **A:** *How's school going?*
> **B:** *OK, but I have two big exams this week.* ***How are things with you?***

B. Now listen to other conversations and circle the follow-up question you hear.

1. **a.** How about you?
   b. What about you?

2. **a.** How about you?
   b. What about you?

3. **a.** What about you?
   b. What are you doing?

4. **a.** How are things?
   b. How are things with you?

⑤ AFTER YOU LISTEN

A. Put these sentences in order to make two conversations. The first one is done for you. Then practice the conversations with a partner.

Conversation 1

___ It's pretty good, thanks. I'm very busy these days. How about you?

___ Yeah, see you later.

_1_ Hi, how are you?

___ Yeah, I'm very busy, too.

___ Well, talk to you later.

___ Fine, thanks. How's school?

Conversation 2

___ Well, have a nice day anyway.

___ Pretty good. It's hot today, isn't it?

_1_ Hi! How's it going?

___ I can't. I have to study.

___ Thanks. You, too.

___ Yeah, I'm going to the pool. How about you?

B. Role-play. You meet a friend in the street. Use this conversation but replace the highlighted parts with expressions in the boxes or your own information.

Greetings	Good-byes
How's it going?	Have a nice day.
How is everything?	See you later.
How have you been?	Talk to you later.
	Bye for now.
	Catch you later.

a baseball game   the pool   the mall
tomorrow   Saturday   next week
brother   friend   mother   father
at a party   at the beach   at school   at home

A: Hi Yu-ting. How's it going?

B: Pretty good. And you?

A: Fine, thanks. Are you going to a movie tonight?

B: No, I'm going to a concert. What about you?

A: I'm meeting my sister downtown.

B: Well, I'd better go. Have a nice day.

A: See you later.

LESSON OBJECTIVES
▸ Recognizing numbers
▸ Spelling e-mail addresses
▸ Asking for clarification

Lesson 1   What's your e-mail address?

1 BEFORE YOU LISTEN

How often do you do these activities? Check (✓) the correct column. Then compare your answers with a partner.

	Every day	Sometimes	Never
1. talk on a cell phone	☐	☐	☐
2. use a public telephone	☐	☐	☐
3. leave a message on someone's voice mail	☐	☐	☐
4. receive a voice-mail message	☐	☐	☐
5. send a text message	☐	☐	☐
6. receive a text message	☐	☐	☐
7. check for e-mail messages	☐	☐	☐
8. send an e-mail	☐	☐	☐
9. receive an e-mail	☐	☐	☐
10. send instant messages	☐	☐	☐

2 LISTEN AND UNDERSTAND 🎧 CD 1 Tracks 11 & 12

A. Customer service clerks are asking for personal information. Listen and write the telephone numbers you hear.

1. home number: _____   work number: _____
2. cell number: _____   home number: _____
3. cell number: _____   weekend number: _____
4. home number: _____   work number: _____

B. Listen to the rest of the conversations. Fix the mistakes in these addresses. The first one is done for you.

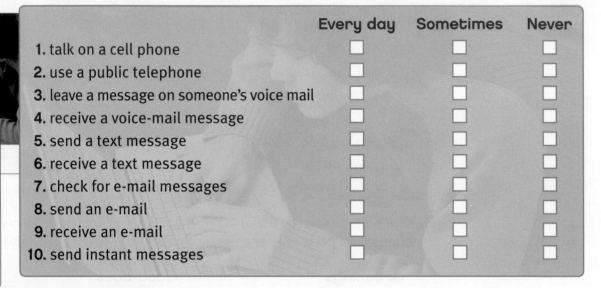

1. 1455 Westbury Avenue _1445_
2. 349 Haig Street, Apartment 66 _____
3. 70 Johnson Street, Apartment B _____
4. 419 Castle Street, Apartment 140 _____

3 LISTEN AND UNDERSTAND CD 1 Track 13

A. People are giving each other their e-mail addresses. Listen and finish writing these e-mail addresses.

1. terrybrown@_____
2. _____@wow.com
3. _____@oneworld.com
4. rosa_____@_____.com

B. Listen again. Are these statements true or false? Write *T* (true) or *F* (false). The first one is done for you.

1. Terry checks her e-mail often. _T_
2. Li-wei's mother suggested his e-mail address. ___
3. Yumi's sister uses e-mail a lot. ___
4. Rosa has her birthday in her e-mail address. ___

4 TUNE IN CD 1 Tracks 14 & 15

A. Listen and notice how people ask for clarification.

> A: *My number is 945-667-0513.*
> B: ***Could you say that again, please?***
>
> A: *My address is 349 Haig Street, Apartment 56.*
> B: ***Did you say*** *339 Haig Street?*
>
> A: *It's 17 Johnson Street, Apartment B.*
> B: ***Is that*** *17 or 70?*

B. Now listen to other conversations. Does the person ask for clarification in each conversation? Check (✓) the correct column.

	Asks for clarification	Does not ask for clarification
1.	☐	☐
2.	☐	☐
3.	☐	☐
4.	☐	☐

AFTER YOU LISTEN

A. Complete one ID card with the information in the boxes. Do not show it to anyone. You can use any of the telephone numbers or street addresses.

1.
Name . . . .
Telephone . . . .
Address . . . .
. . . .
E-mail . . . .

3.
Name . . . .
Telephone . . . .
Address . . . .
. . . .
E-mail . . . .

2.
Name . . . .
Telephone . . . .
Address . . . .
. . . .
E-mail . . . .

4.
Name . . . .
Telephone . . . .
Address . . . .
. . . .
E-mail . . . .

NAMES	TELEPHONE NUMBERS	STREET ADDRESSES	E-MAIL ADDRESSES
Scarlet Jones	782-328-4608	33 West 33rd Street	jp@notmail.com
BB Tanaka	230-591-3329	49 Green Street	katy@wow.com
Katy Wyman	945-221-6975	15 Castle Road	lihong@galaxy.com
Li-hong Su	230-917-6875	43 West 33rd Street	happy@harmoni.com
Jae-won Park	782-598-4380	50 Castle Road	red@yohoo.com
PJ Jones	945-392-4163	2634 George Street	jones@oneworld.com

B. Find three people who completed the other three ID cards using this conversation. Replace the highlighted parts with information in the boxes. Guess which ID card each person chose and then complete it.

A: *What's your name?*
B: *It's Katy Wyman.*
A: *Could you say that again, please?*
B: *Sure. Katy Wyman.*
A: *Thanks. And do you have a telephone number?*
B: *Yes, it's 230-591-3329.*
A: *And what's your street address?*
B: *It's 33 West 33rd Street.*
A: *Did you say 43 West 33rd Street?*

B: *No, it's 33 West 33rd Street.*
A: *Do you have an e-mail address?*
B: *Uh-huh. It's katy@wow.com.*
A: *Sorry, could you say that again?*
B: *katy@wow.com*
A: *Thanks. Are you ID card 4?*
B: *No, I'm ID card 1.*

LESSON OBJECTIVES

▸ Recognizing ways of using the telephone
▸ Identifying people's purposes
▸ Using rising and falling intonation

Lesson 2 May I speak to Tony, please?

① BEFORE YOU LISTEN

When do you use these telephone expressions? Check (✓) the correct column. Then compare your answers with a partner.

	Answer the telephone	Ask to speak to someone	Explain where someone is
1. Hello. This is Justin speaking.	☐	☐	☐
2. I'm sorry. He can't come to the phone.	☐	☐	☐
3. I'd like to speak to Samantha, please.	☐	☐	☐
4. Smith Enterprises. Emma speaking.	☐	☐	☐
5. I'm afraid she's busy at the moment.	☐	☐	☐
6. Is Pei-ting there, please?	☐	☐	☐
7. Sorry, she's not here right now.	☐	☐	☐
8. May I speak to Sang-woo, please?	☐	☐	☐
9. He'll be back soon.	☐	☐	☐
10. Totem Records. Can I help you?	☐	☐	☐

② LISTEN AND UNDERSTAND 🎧 CD 1 Track 16

A. People are making telephone calls. What do they do? Listen and circle the correct answer.

1. **Cindy** a. leaves a message   b. offers to call back later
2. **Tina** a. waits for Allison to come to the phone   b. offers to call back later
3. **Jack** a. waits for Moe to come to the phone   b. leaves a message
4. **Tim** a. leaves a message   b. offers to call back later
5. **Billy** a. waits for Hao-ming to come to the phone b. offers to call back later

B. Listen again. Are these statements true or false? Write T (true) or F (false).

1. Cindy's number is 735-744-3339. ___
2. Allison will be home by six o'clock. ___
3. Jack is in Moe's English class. ___
4. Mei-ling already has Tim's phone number. ___
5. Hao-ming and Billy live in the same apartment. ___

3 LISTEN AND UNDERSTAND 🎧 CD 1 Track 17

A. People are leaving voice-mail messages. Is each message a request, a reminder, a thank-you, or an apology? Listen and ⟨circle⟩ the correct answer.

1. **a.** an apology   **b.** a reminder
2. **a.** an apology   **b.** a request
3. **a.** a thank-you   **b.** a request
4. **a.** a thank-you   **b.** a reminder
5. **a.** a request   **b.** an apology

B. Listen again. Check (✓) the correct statement. The first one is done for you.

1. **a.** The concert is on Friday at 6:00. ___
   b. They will meet in front of the theater at 4:45. ✓
2. **a.** Koichi's birthday was on Saturday. ___
   b. Sarah went to the airport with her sister. ___
3. **a.** Jian-hao wants to borrow a laptop. ___
   b. Jian-hao is doing a biology project. ___
4. **a.** Ricardo enjoyed the party. ___
   b. Ricardo gave Anna a ride home. ___
5. **a.** Kevin is going to buy a new computer. ___
   b. Kevin's computer is being fixed. ___

4 TUNE IN 🎧 CD 1 Tracks 18 & 19

A. Listen and notice how people use falling and rising intonation to ask for information and check information.

We use falling intonation when we ask for information.

A: **What time will you call?** ↘
B: About six o'clock.

A: **Who's calling, please?** ↘
B: My name's Jack. I'm in her biology class.

We use rising intonation when we check information.

A: Please ask her to call Cindy.
B: Sorry, **did you say Cindy?** ↗

A: **Is this Billy?** ↗
B: Yes, but don't worry, thanks. I'll call him back later.

B. Now listen to other people. Does each person ask for information or check information? ⟨Circle⟩ the correct answer.

1. **a.** asks   **b.** checks
2. **a.** asks   **b.** checks
3. **a.** asks   **b.** checks
4. **a.** asks   **b.** checks
5. **a.** asks   **b.** checks

5 AFTER YOU LISTEN

A. Put these sentences in order to make a telephone conversation. The first one is done for you. Then practice the conversation with a partner.

___ I think so, but anyway it's 930-441-7689.

___ Yes, that's right.

___ I see. Could I leave a message?

___ Did you say 930-441-7689?

___ Thank you very much. Good-bye.

___ Hi, Kazu. This is Margaret. May I speak to Rosa, please?

___ Around seven o'clock. OK. Does she have your number?

___ All right. I'll give her the message.

___ Yes, of course.

_1_ Hello. Kazu speaking.

___ Please ask her to call me tonight around seven o'clock.

___ Sorry, Margaret. She's not here right now.

___ Bye, Margaret.

B. Role-play. You are calling a friend who is not at home. Work with a partner. Take turns asking to speak to your friend and leaving a message. Use this conversation but replace the highlighted parts with your own information. Write your partner's message below.

A: *Hello.*

B: *Hello. May I speak to Elizabeth, please?*

A: *Sorry, she isn't here right now.*

B: *When will she be back?*

A: *In about an hour. Do you want to leave a message?*

B: *Yes, please. This is Michael. Please ask her to call me.*

A: *OK. And what's your telephone number?*

B: *My cell phone number is 821-997-4566.*

A: *All right. I'll ask her to call you.*

Hey _____,
_____ called.
Please _____
_____
_____
The number is _____
_____.

Unit 3 Telling Time

Lesson 1 What time do you get up?

LESSON OBJECTIVES
▸ Identifying time of day
▸ Understanding work routines
▸ Confirming or correcting information

1 BEFORE YOU LISTEN

How do you say these times? Match each picture with an expression in column A and an expression in column B. The first one is done for you. Then compare your answers with a partner.

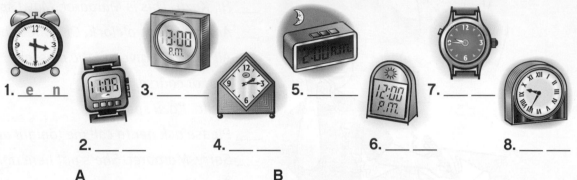

1. _e_ _n_
2. ___ ___
3. ___ ___
4. ___ ___
5. ___ ___
6. ___ ___
7. ___ ___
8. ___ ___

A	B
a. nine thirty-five	**i.** five after eleven
b. two fifteen	**j.** three o'clock in the afternoon
c. nine forty-five	**k.** noon
d. three P.M.	**l.** twenty-five to ten
e. three thirty	**m.** a quarter after two
f. twelve P.M.	**n.** half past three
g. two A.M.	**o.** two o'clock in the morning
h. eleven oh five	**p.** a quarter to ten

2 LISTEN AND UNDERSTAND 🎧 CD 1 Track 20

A. People are talking about their travel plans. Are they at an airport, a train station, or a bus station? Listen and check (✓) the correct column.

	Airport	Train station	Bus station
1.	☐	☐	☐
2.	☐	☐	☐
3.	☐	☐	☐
4.	☐	☐	☐

B. Listen again. Circle the correct time.

1. **a.** 2:15   **b.** 2:50
2. **a.** 3:13   **b.** 3:30
3. **a.** 4:15   **b.** 4:50
4. **a.** 11:05   **b.** 5:11

③ LISTEN AND UNDERSTAND  CD 1 Track 21

A. Students in an evening class are talking about their work. What do they do? Listen and number these people from 1 to 4.

a. a teacher ___

b. a taxi driver ___

c. a musician ___

d. a supermarket cashier ___

B. Listen again. When does each person start and finish work? Write the times you hear in each conversation.

	Starts	Finishes
1.	_____	_____
2.	_____	_____
3.	_____	_____
4.	_____	_____

④ TUNE IN 🎧 CD 1 Tracks 22 & 23

A. Listen and notice how people confirm or correct information.

Confirm information	Correct information
A: *Did she say 2:15?* **B:** ***That's right.***	**A:** *Oh, no. Our flight is 30 minutes late.* **B:** *I think he said 20 minutes,* ***actually***.
A: *So you get home pretty early, then?* **B:** ***Yeah, I do.***	**A:** *So you work for 12 hours at a time?* **B:** ***No***, *about 10 hours,* ***actually***.

B. Now listen to other conversations. Does the person confirm information or correct information in each conversation? Check (✓) the correct column.

	Confirm information	Correct information
1.	☐	☐
2.	☐	☐
3.	☐	☐
4.	☐	☐
5.	☐	☐

⑤ AFTER YOU LISTEN

A. Match each question with its answer. Then practice the conversations with a partner.

1. Did she say the bus leaves at ten after ten? ____
2. Does your class start at 9:15? ____
3. So you study 12 hours a day? ____
4. So you finish work at 3:00 A.M.? ____
5. The movie starts at 11:30 P.M., right? ____

a. No, about 14 hours, actually.
b. No, she said it leaves at 9:50.
c. Correct. Three o'clock in the morning.
d. Yes, that's right. A quarter after nine.
e. No, at 11:30 in the morning.

B. What is your schedule like on school days? Complete the survey for yourself. Add two more questions of your own and answer them.

	Me	My partner
1. What time do you usually get up?	_____	_____
2. What time do you have breakfast?	_____	_____
3. What time do you leave home?	_____	_____
4. When do you usually arrive back home?	_____	_____
5. What time do you eat dinner?	_____	_____
6. When do you usually go to bed?	_____	_____
7. _____	_____	_____
8. _____	_____	_____

C. Work with a partner. Take turns asking and answering the questions and complete the survey for your partner. How many of your answers are the same?

Lesson 2 Are you free on Friday night?

1 BEFORE YOU LISTEN

Check (✓) the activities in the list you are going to do this week. Write the day of the week you are going to do each activity. Then compare your answers with a partner.

Monday	Tuesday	Wednesday	Thursday	Friday	Saturday	Sunday

1. go to a movie ☐ _____
2. go dancing ☐ _____
3. go out for lunch ☐ _____
4. go to a party ☐ _____
5. get a haircut ☐ _____
6. go skateboarding ☐ _____
7. do karate ☐ _____
8. go shopping ☐ _____
9. have a barbecue ☐ _____
10. watch a DVD ☐ _____

2 LISTEN AND UNDERSTAND 🎧 CD 1 Track 24

A. Josh is planning a surprise party for his friend Naoko. Listen and check (✓) the nights each person is free. Then answer the question.

	Wednesday	Thursday	Friday	Saturday
1. Carlos	☐	☐	☐	☐
2. Ai	☐	☐	☐	☐
3. Jane	☐	☐	☐	☐

Which night is everybody free? _____

B. Listen again. Match each person with the correct activity.

1. Carlos ____   **a.** studies Korean
2. Ai ____   **b.** works on Friday nights
3. Jane ____   **c.** does karate

3 LISTEN AND UNDERSTAND 🎧 CD 1 Track 25

A. Friends are leaving voice-mail messages about meeting up. Does each caller give information about *when* to meet or *where* to meet? Listen and check (✓) the correct column.

	When to meet	Where to meet
1.	☐	☐
2.	☐	☐
3.	☐	☐
4.	☐	☐

B. Listen again. Circle the two topics you hear in each message.

1. **a.** her wedding
   b. the weather
   c. her trip

2. **a.** a store
   b. prices
   c. clothing

3. **a.** a meal
   b. music
   c. the weather

4. **a.** a famous person
   b. clothing
   c. a meal

4 TUNE IN 🎧 CD 1 Tracks 26 & 27

A. Listen and notice how people give polite negative answers.

> **A:** *How about Friday?*
> **B:** ***Unfortunately,*** *I work every Friday night.*
>
> **A:** *And is Friday night good for you?*
> **B:** ***Not really, I'm afraid. The problem is*** *I have karate on Fridays.*
>
> **A:** *Are you free on Saturday night?*
> **B:** ***I'm afraid not. The thing is*** *I have Korean classes on Wednesday and Saturday evenings.*

B. Now listen to other conversations and circle the polite negative answer you hear.

1. **a.** unfortunately   **b.** the problem is
2. **a.** I'm afraid not   **b.** not really, I'm afraid
3. **a.** unfortunately   **b.** the thing is
4. **a.** the thing is   **b.** the problem is

5 AFTER YOU LISTEN

A. You are planning your weekend. Choose four activities in the box and write them in your planner.

| go to a movie | go out for lunch | play tennis | watch a basketball game |
| go shopping | have a barbecue | watch a DVD | go dancing |

	Friday	Saturday	Sunday
		Day	
Morning			
Afternoon			
Evening			

Planner

◀ Day Week Month ▶

B. Work with a partner. Take turns inviting your partner to do the activities with you at the times in your planner. If your partner is busy, ask about another time and activity. Use these conversations but replace the highlighted parts . How many activities are you going to do together?

A: *Are you free on Friday evening?*
B: *Yes, I'm not doing anything.*
A: *Would you like to go to a movie?*
B: *Sure. That sounds nice.*

A: *Are you free on Saturday morning?*
B: *No, I'm afraid not. I'm planning to play tennis.*
A: *Oh. Well, how about Saturday afternoon? Are you free then?*
B: *Yeah, I am.*
A: *Would you like to watch a basketball game with me?*
B: *Yeah, that would be great.*

LESSON OBJECTIVES
- Identifying prices
- Identifying items in a store
- Using the contraction of *did you*

Lesson 1   How much does it cost?

1 BEFORE YOU LISTEN

How much do you think these items cost in New York City? Match each item with its price. Then compare your answers with a partner.

1. a can of soda	_____	a.	$299.00
2. a digital camera	_____	b.	$199.99
3. a skateboard	_____	c.	$135.00
4. a magazine	_____	d.	$44.99
5. a movie ticket	_____	e.	$25.00
6. a cell phone	_____	f.	$16.99
7. a T-shirt	_____	g.	$12.95
8. jeans	_____	h.	$10.00
9. sandals	_____	i.	$4.50
10. a comic book	_____	j.	80¢

2 LISTEN AND UNDERSTAND 🎧 CD 1 Track 28

A. Friends are talking about their shopping. Listen and circle the correct price of each item.

1.	a. jeans	$85.00 $25.00	c. sandals	$99.00 $90.00
	b. a T-shirt	$49.00 $29.00	d. sunglasses	$38.00 $108.00
2.	a. DVDs	$50.00 $15.00	c. CDs	$4.00 $24.00
	b. a video game	$12.00 $20.00	d. a CD rack	$19.00 $15.00
3.	a. magazines	$10.00 $10.25	c. a dictionary	$7.95 $5.75
	b. Harry Potter books	$99.00 $19.99	d. comic books	$70.00 $17.50

B. Listen again. Was each person happy or unhappy with the prices? Check (✓) the correct column.

	Happy	Unhappy
1.	☐	☐
2.	☐	☐
3.	☐	☐

3 LISTEN AND UNDERSTAND 🎧 CD 1 Track 29

A. People are in a store. What are they buying? Listen and number these items from 1 to 4.

a. ____

c. ____

b. ____

d. ____

B. Listen again. Did customers get the correct change? Check (✓) the correct column.

	Yes	No
1.	☐	☐
2.	☐	☐
3.	☐	☐
4.	☐	☐

4 TUNE IN 🎧 CD 1 Tracks 30 & 31

A. Listen and notice how people contract *did you* in questions so it sounds like *didja*.

did you	*didja*
So how much **did you** spend today, Elizabeth? = So how much **didja** spend today, Elizabeth?
Where **did you** go? = Where **didja** go?

B. Now listen to short conversations. Is the question with *did you* contracted or not? Check (✓) the correct column.

	did you	*didja*
1.	☐	☐
2.	☐	☐
3.	☐	☐
4.	☐	☐

⑤ AFTER YOU LISTEN

A. Work with a partner. Decide who is student A and who is student B. Write prices for your items. Do not let your partner see them.

Student A:

| cap $ _____ | can of soda $ _____ | comic book $ _____ | T-shirt $ _____ |

Student B:

| laptop $ _____ | cell phone $ _____ | sneakers $ _____ | jeans $ _____ |

B. Ask each other how much the items in part A cost. Use this conversation but replace the highlighted parts with expressions in the box and your own information.

A: *How much is the cap?*
B: *It's $49.95.*
A: *How much did you say?*
B: *$49.95.*
A: *That's expensive.*

> *That's expensive.*
> *That's not bad.*
> *That's pretty cheap.*

C. Role-play. You are at a store. Take turns being a store clerk and a customer. The clerk gives a price for each item (less than $100). The customer has $100 to spend. Use this conversation but replace the highlighted parts with these items and your own information.

digital camera   cap   T-shirt   computer game

cell phone   DVD   comic book   skateboard

A: *I'm interested in this digital camera. How much is it?*
B: *It's on sale this week. It's usually $250, but this week it's only $98.99.*
A: *That's pretty cheap. I'll take it, please.*
B: *Certainly. And how will you pay for that?*
A: *Cash. Here's $100.*
B: *Thank you. And here's your change. $1.00.*
A: *Sorry, how much did you say? I think you made a mistake.*
B: *Sorry, it should be $1.01. Here's your penny.*

LESSON OBJECTIVES
▸ Identifying stores
▸ Identifying locations in a store
▸ Making and responding to suggestions

Lesson 2 It's just what I need!

1 BEFORE YOU LISTEN

A. Where can you buy these items? Write each item under the correct store. Then compare your answers with a partner.

| a magazine | a digital camera | a golf ball | a donut |
| a cookie | a TV | a comic book | a baseball cap |

Electronics Store	Bookstore	Sporting Goods Store	Bakery
_____	_____	_____	_____
_____	_____	_____	_____
_____	_____	_____	_____
_____	_____	_____	_____

B. Work with a partner. What are two other items you can buy in each store? Write them in the correct columns.

2 LISTEN AND UNDERSTAND 🎧 CD 1 Track 32

A. Friends are shopping. What kind of store are they in? Listen and number these stores from 1 to 4.

a. a sporting goods store ___

b. a bookstore ___

c. a music store ___

d. a bakery ___

B. Listen again. Do the people buy anything? Check (✓) the correct column.

	Yes	No
1.	☐	☐
2.	☐	☐
3.	☐	☐
4.	☐	☐

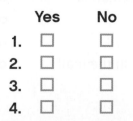

3 LISTEN AND UNDERSTAND CD 1 Track 33

A. A department store is making announcements about its sales. Where can you find these items? Listen and **circle** the correct floor number.

1. a children's game   **a.** 5   **b.** 4

2. a gift for a golfer   **a.** 5   **b.** 3

3. a French magazine   **a.** 4   **b.** 2

4. a new DVD player   **a.** 3   **b.** 2

B. Listen again. Match each statement with the correct item.

1. You can buy these for $29.95 today. ___

2. These cost less than $20.00 this week. ___

3. One of these is free if you spend more than $30.00. ___

4. These are 40% off this week. ___

a. digital cameras
b. books
c. T-shirts
d. computer games

4 TUNE IN CD 1 Tracks 34 & 35

A. Listen and notice how people make and respond to suggestions.

Suggestions	Accept	Decline
Why don't we each get one?	*That's a good idea.*	
Why don't you try them on?	*I think I will.*	
Maybe you'd like to sit down.	*Great idea!*	
Maybe we could ask for a bigger size.		*I don't think so.*
How about a new computer game?		*I'm not sure.*
Maybe you could get a digital camera.		*Probably not.*

B. Now listen to people giving suggestions. Does the other person accept or decline the suggestion in each conversation? **Circle** the correct answer.

1. How about a DVD?   **a.** accepts   **b.** declines

2. Maybe you could buy her some chocolates.   **a.** accepts   **b.** declines

3. How about a tie?   **a.** accepts   **b.** declines

4. Maybe we could get some Korean food.   **a.** accepts   **b.** declines

5. Why don't you go to that new store in the mall?   **a.** accepts   **b.** declines

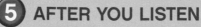

5 AFTER YOU LISTEN

A. What are good gifts to buy? Think of three suitable birthday gifts for these people.
Use the gifts in the box or your own ideas. Write them in each person's column.

flowers	a digital camera	chocolates	a book	a computer game
a bicycle	an MP3 player	a puzzle	a DVD	a skateboard

1. **a 13-year-old brother**

_____

_____

_____

2. **a 19-year-old girlfriend**

_____

_____

_____

3. **a math teacher**

_____

_____

_____

B. Role-play. You are discussing gifts for the people in part A. Take turns making and responding to
suggestions. Use this conversation but replace the highlighted parts with the information in part A
and your own ideas.

A: *I'd like to buy a gift for my* brother .

B: *Why don't you buy* him flowers?

A: *Mm. No, I don't think so.*

B: *Well, maybe* he'd like a skateboard.

A: *I'm not sure.*

B: *How about buying* him an MP3 player?

A: *Yeah. That's a good idea. Thanks for the suggestion.*

Unit 5 Dates & Events

LESSON OBJECTIVES
› Understanding people's plans
› Understanding descriptions of events
› Showing interest

Lesson 1   When's your birthday?

① BEFORE YOU LISTEN

A. Number the months in order from 1 to 12.

___ October	___ August	___ April	___ December
___ June	___ May	___ February	___ September
___ March	___ November	___ July	___ January

B. When do these people have their birthday? Write the month and day. Use this form:
August 16. **Then compare your answers with a partner.**

Birthday

1. Me _____
2. Father _____
3. Mother _____
4. Brother or sister _____
5. Best friend _____

② LISTEN AND UNDERSTAND 🎧 CD 1 Track 36

A. People are talking about their birthdays. Have they already had their birthdays this year? Listen and check (✓) the correct column.

	Has already had it	Has not had it yet
1.	☐	☐
2.	☐	☐
3.	☐	☐
4.	☐	☐
5.	☐	☐

B. Listen again. Match each person with the correct celebration.

1. Andrew ___   **a.** a party at home with friends
2. Yumi ___   **b.** a family celebration at home
3. Linda ___   **c.** a trip to Wonder World
4. Akihiko ___   **d.** a barbecue at the park
5. Katy ___   **e.** lunch at a seafood cafe

3 LISTEN AND UNDERSTAND 🎧 CD 1 Track 37

A. Emily is talking to Jin-won about her school. Listen and write the dates for these school events. Use this form: **8/16**. The first one is done for you.

1. First semester <u>8/16–12/17</u>

2. Second semester _____

3. International Festival _____

4. Sports Festival _____

5. School Exchange Day _____

6. Music Gala _____

7. International Trip _____

Emily and Jin-won

B. Listen again. Are these statements true or false? Write *T* (true) or *F* (false).

1. Emily and Jin-won have summer vacation in June and July. ___

2. Students can win prizes at the International Festival. ___

3. Other schools take part in the Sports Festival. ___

4. The Music Gala lasts for three days. ___

5. Emily hated the trip to Malaysia. ___

4 TUNE IN 🎧 CD 1 Tracks 38 & 39

A. Listen and notice how people show interest in what someone is saying.

> **A:** *My parents gave me a new scooter.*
> **B:** *Oh, that's cool.*
>
> **A:** *My birthday is on Saturday.*
> **B:** *Oh, great. What have you got planned?*
>
> **A:** *My family's going to have a barbecue.*
> **B:** *That sounds nice.*
>
> **A:** *All the schools get together for a huge sports competition.*
> **B:** *How exciting!*

B. Now listen to other conversations and circle the expression of interest you hear.

1. **a.** How exciting!
   b. How nice!

2. **a.** Oh, that's interesting.
   b. Oh, that's cool.

3. **a.** Oh, that's nice.
   b. That sounds nice.

4. **a.** Great!
   b. That's great!

(5) AFTER YOU LISTEN

A. Complete the conversation with expressions in the box. Then practice the conversation with a partner.

> Oh, that's cool!   How exciting!   That sounds nice.

A: *Do you have any plans for your birthday?*

B: *My boyfriend and I are going to my favorite restaurant in Chinatown.*

A: _____ *Are you doing anything after that?*

B: *We're going to that new club downtown. My brother works there, so he can get us in for free.*

A: _____ *They have great bands, don't they?*

B: *Yeah, and quite a few movie stars go there.*

A: _____ *Lucky you!*

B. What do you do on your birthday? Complete this survey for yourself. Use expressions in the box and your own information.

> have a family meal at home   go out to eat in a restaurant
>
> sing "Happy Birthday"   have a party
>
> go somewhere special   play games
>
> have a birthday cake with candles

	Me	My partner
1. When is your birthday?	_____	_____
2. How does your family celebrate birthdays?	_____	_____
3. How do your friends celebrate birthdays?	_____	_____
4. What are you going to do for your next birthday?	_____	_____
5. What gift would you like to get for your next birthday?	_____	_____

C. Work with a partner. Take turns asking and answering the questions and complete the survey for your partner. How many of your answers are the same?

LESSON OBJECTIVES
▸ Recognizing dates
▸ Understanding descriptions of events
▸ Using intonation in questions

Lesson 2 So when was that?

① BEFORE YOU LISTEN

Work with a partner. When did these events from Tiger Woods' life happen? Match each year with its event. Then check your answers below.

1. 1975 ___
2. 1991 ___
3. 1996 ___
4. 1997 ___
5. 2004 ___

a. He became a professional golfer.
b. He got married.
c. He was born.
d. He won his first major professional championship.
e. He became the youngest player to win the US Junior Amateur Championship.

② LISTEN AND UNDERSTAND CD 1 Track 40

A. People are taking part in a quiz show about movie stars. Listen and write the correct year for each event.

Event	Year
1. Ziyi Zhang was born.	_____
2. The movie *House of Flying Daggers* came out.	_____
3. Tom Cruise was born.	_____
4. The movie *Risky Business* came out.	_____
5. Nicole Kidman was born.	_____

B. Listen again. Are these statements true or false? Write *T* (true) or *F* (false).

1. Ziyi Zhang was born in Shanghai. ___
2. Tom Cruise was born in Syracuse, New York. ___
3. Tom Cruise's first big film was *War of the Worlds*. ___
4. Nicole Kidman and Tom Cruise were married for about ten years. ___
5. Nicole Kidman was born in Australia. ___

ANSWERS: 1. c, 2. e, 3. a, 4. d, 5. b

③ LISTEN AND UNDERSTAND 🎧 CD 1 Track 41

A. Brian is writing a magazine article about some people who attended his high school. Listen and number the events for each person from 1 to 4.

1. Sue
- **a.** graduated from school ___
- **b.** won an Olympic medal ___
- **c.** moved to Boston ___
- **d.** went to Mexico ___

2. Jae-won
- **a.** recorded a CD ___
- **b.** won a music contest ___
- **c.** learned to play the guitar ___
- **d.** left school ___

3. Laura
- **a.** lived in Italy ___
- **b.** worked for a newspaper ___
- **c.** became a TV show host ___
- **d.** studied drama ___

B. Listen again. Check (✓) the correct statement.

Laura

1. **a.** Sue speaks Spanish. ___
   b. Sue worked at the Olympic Games. ___

2. **a.** Jae-won's first CD sold very well. ___
   b. Jae-won is a college graduate. ___

3. **a.** Laura didn't like college. ___
   b. Laura's TV show is popular. ___

④ TUNE IN 🎧 CD 1 Tracks 42 & 43

A. Listen and notice how people use falling and rising intonation in questions.

> **We use falling intonation when we ask a *wh-* question.**
>
> *When was he born?*
>
> *How did you learn to play the guitar?*
>
> *What did you study in college?*
>
> **We use rising intonation when we ask a *yes/no* question.**
>
> *Are you ready?*
>
> *Have you always lived in Boston?*
>
> *Is it interesting to host a TV show?*

B. Now listen to short conversations. Do you hear a question with falling or rising intonation in each conversation? Circle the correct answer.

1. a. ↘   b. ↗
2. a. ↘   b. ↗
3. a. ↘   b. ↗
4. a. ↘   b. ↗

A. Role-play. You are interviewing the actress Gwyneth Paltrow. Match these questions with the correct answers. Then practice the conversation with a partner.

1. So when were you born? ___
2. Where did you grow up? ___
3. How did you learn to act? ___
4. When did you win an Oscar? ___
5. When did you get married? ___
6. When was your first child born? ___

a. In Los Angeles, until I was 11.
b. That was in 2003.
c. I was born in 1972.
d. I learned acting from my parents.
e. She was born in 2004.
f. I got it in 1999 for the movie *Shakespeare in Love.*

B. What are some events in your life? Complete this survey for yourself. Add two more questions of your own and answer them.

	Me	My partner
1. When were you born?	_____	_____
2. Are you an only child?	_____	_____
3. What year did you start elementary school?	_____	_____
4. What year did you start high school?	_____	_____
5. What year did you start learning English?	_____	_____
6. Are you studying other subjects?	_____	_____
7. _____?	_____	_____
8. _____?	_____	_____

C. Work with a partner. Take turns asking and answering the questions and complete the survey for your partner. How many of your answers are the same?

LESSON OBJECTIVES
- Understanding descriptions of places
- Distinguishing facts and opinions
- Expressing agreement

Lesson 1   It sounds like an interesting place

1 BEFORE YOU LISTEN

A. Can you find these items in the picture? Number them from 1 to 8.

1. a statue
2. a playground
3. a shopping mall
4. a swimming pool
5. a train station
6. a snack bar
7. a museum
8. a park

B. What are three interesting places near where you live? Write their names. Then compare your answers with a partner.

1. _____
2. _____
3. _____

2 LISTEN AND UNDERSTAND 🎧 CD 2 Track 02

A. Tour guides are describing different places. What do they say about each place? Listen and check (✓) the two topics you hear in each description.

1. the lake	a. name ___	b. age ___	c. size ___
2. the temple	a. cost ___	b. age ___	c. size ___
3. the tower	a. cost ___	b. height ___	c. view ___

B. Listen again. Are these statements true or false? Write *T* (true) or *F* (false).

1. Lake Biwa is beautiful but very small. ___
2. Wat Chiang Man is the oldest temple in Chiang Mai. ___
3. You can eat at the Menara Kuala Lumpur tower. ___

Menara Kuala Lumpur

Lake Biwa

Wat Chiang Man

3 LISTEN AND UNDERSTAND  CD 2 Track 03

A. People are asking Max about different places in his city. Does he state facts or give opinions? Listen and check (✓) the correct column.

	Facts	Opinions
1.	☐	☐
2.	☐	☐
3.	☐	☐
4.	☐	☐

B. Listen again. Circle the correct information. The first one is done for you.

1. The park is *in front of /* behind the train station.
2. The mall has some *great / expensive* stores.
3. Max likes to shop *downtown / at the mall*.
4. Max says modern paintings are *very interesting / horrible*.

4 TUNE IN CD 2 Tracks 04 & 05

A. Listen and notice how people express agreement with affirmative and negative statements.

Affirmative Statements	Negative Statements
A: *It's beautiful.* B: **Yes, it is.**	A: *It's not very big.* B: **No, it isn't.**
A: *The water's very clear.* B: **Yes, it is.**	A: *They're not expensive.* B: **No, they're not.**
A: *It probably has good restaurants, too.* B: **Yeah, it does.**	A: *I guess you don't like modern paintings.* B: **No, I don't.**

B. Now listen to other statements. How can you agree with each one? Circle the correct response.

1. **a.** Yes, it is.   **b.** No, it isn't.
2. **a.** Yes, it does.   **b.** No, it doesn't.
3. **a.** Yes, it is.   **b.** No, it isn't.
4. **a.** Yes, they are.   **b.** No, they aren't.
5. **a.** Yeah, it is.   **b.** No, it isn't.
6. **a.** Yeah, it is.   **b.** No, it isn't.

5 AFTER YOU LISTEN

A. Work with a partner. Decide who is student A and who is student B. Individually, complete your survey about the capital city in your country. Add two more places and check (✓) the correct column.

Student A	Worth visiting	Not worth visiting
1. the science museum	☐	☐
2. the train station	☐	☐
3. the main sports stadium	☐	☐
4. the main park	☐	☐
5. _____	☐	☐
6. _____	☐	☐

Student B	Worth visiting	Not worth visiting
1. the zoo	☐	☐
2. the art museum	☐	☐
3. the airport	☐	☐
4. the main shopping area	☐	☐
5. _____	☐	☐
6. _____	☐	☐

B. Take turns asking and answering questions about the places in each survey. Use these conversations but replace the highlighted parts with words in the box and your own information.

interesting	beautiful	great	unusual
nice	not very interesting	boring	ugly

A: *What do you think of the zoo?*
B: *It's great.*
A: *So it's worth visiting?*
B: *Yes, it is.*

B: *What do you think of the science museum?*
A: *It's boring.*
B: *So it's not worth visiting?*
A: *No, not really.*

C. Decide with your partner: Which place in your capital city is the most interesting?

Lesson 2 How do I get there?

1 BEFORE YOU LISTEN

Follow these directions on the map. Write the places you find. Then compare your answers with a partner.

1. Go one block on First Street and turn right on King Street. It's on your left.

   _____

2. Go one block on First Street and turn right on King Street. It's on your right.

   _____

3. Go two blocks on First Street and turn right on Queen Street. It's on your left.

   _____

4. Go one block on First Street and turn left on King Street. It's on your right.

   _____

5. Go two blocks on First Street and turn left on Queen Street. It's on your right.

   _____

2 LISTEN AND UNDERSTAND 🎧 CD 2 Track 06

A. People are asking for information. Where are they? Listen and number these places from 1 to 5.

a. in an office building ____
b. in a shopping mall ____
c. on a street ____
d. on a college campus ____
e. at an airport ____

**B. Listen again. Are these statements true or false?
Write T (true) or F (false).**

1. The woman is looking for the computer center. ____
2. The man will need to take the elevator. ____
3. The man likes the ice-cream parlor on the third floor better. ____
4. The music store is next to a sporting goods store. ____
5. The woman needs to go downstairs. ____

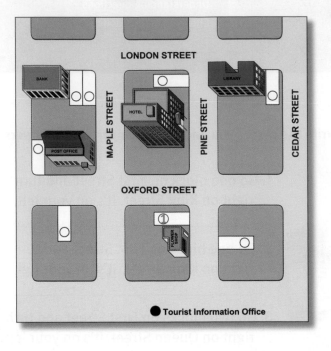

A. People are asking for directions at a tourist information office. Listen and number the places they want to go on the map. The first one is done for you.

1. a coffee shop
2. a hairdresser
3. a music store
4. a noodle shop

B. Listen again. What does the clerk at the tourist office like about each place? Check (✓) the correct column.

	Quality	Service	Price
1.	☐	☐	☐
2.	☐	☐	☐
3.	☐	☐	☐
4.	☐	☐	☐

4 **TUNE IN** 🎧 CD 2 Tracks 08 & 09

A. Listen and notice how people check understanding by questioning or repeating what has been said.

Questioning

A: *Turn left on Pine and you'll see Bob's Coffee Shop on the left, next to a flower shop.*
B: *Did you say Pine Street or Green Street?*

Repeating

A: *Turn left on Oxford. The hairdresser will be on the left, across from the post office.*
B: *On Oxford Street, across from the post office.*

B. Now listen to how other people check understanding. Does the person check understanding by questioning or repeating what has been said in each conversation? Circle the correct answer.

1. **a.** questioning   **b.** repeating
2. **a.** questioning   **b.** repeating
3. **a.** questioning   **b.** repeating
4. **a.** questioning   **b.** repeating
5. **a.** questioning   **b.** repeating

A. Work with a partner. Decide who is student A and who is student B. Individually, mark these places on your map. Do not let your partner see them.

> **Student A:** Bicycle World, Comics Corner, Metro Music
> **Student B:** Century Computers, Universal Sports, Top Jeans

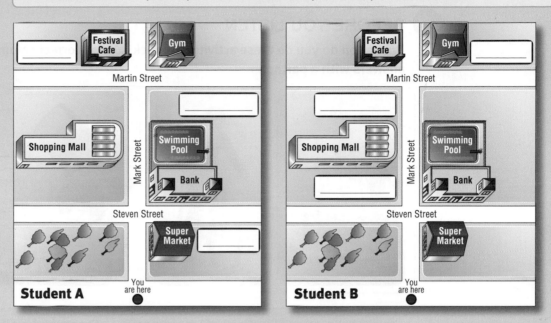

B. Take turns asking about and giving directions to the places on the maps. Use this conversation but replace the highlighted parts with information from your own map. Give directions from "You are here." Write the new places on your map.

> **Student A ask for directions to:** Century Computers, Universal Sports, Top Jeans
> **Student B ask for directions to:** Bicycle World, Comics Corner, Metro Music

A: *Excuse me. I'm trying to find Century Computers. Do you know where it is, please?*

B: *Yes. Just go straight ahead.*

A: *Uh-huh.*

B: *And then turn right on Martin Street. Century Computers is on the left.*

A: *Sorry. Did you say turn left or turn right?*

B: *Um. Turn right.*

A: *OK. So turn right on Martin Street, and it's on the left?*

B: *Correct. It's next to the gym.*

A: *Thanks a lot.*

B: *No problem.*

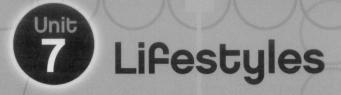

Unit 7 Lifestyles

LESSON OBJECTIVES
▸ Understanding activities and routines
▸ Recognizing likes and dislikes
▸ Using double questions

Lesson 1   Do you ride every day?

1 **BEFORE YOU LISTEN**

How often do you do these activities? Check (✓) the correct column. Then compare your answers with a partner.

	Every day	Once a week	Never
1. surf the Internet	☐	☐	☐
2. ride a bike	☐	☐	☐
3. send text messages	☐	☐	☐
4. play sports	☐	☐	☐
5. watch DVDs	☐	☐	☐
6. listen to music	☐	☐	☐
7. read comic books	☐	☐	☐
8. play computer games	☐	☐	☐

2 **LISTEN AND UNDERSTAND** 🎧 CD 2 Track 10

A. School friends are talking about their daily activities. Listen and number these topics from 1 to 4.

a. watching DVDs ___

b. cycling ___

c. surfing the Internet ___

d. sending text messages ___

B. Listen again. Are these statements true or false? Write *T* (true) or *F* (false).

1. Soo-ji likes a Web site about pop stars and movie stars. ___

2. Josh often makes phone calls. ___

3. Peter has a small collection of DVDs. ___

4. Kate stays home when it's cold or wet. ___

3 LISTEN AND UNDERSTAND CD 2 Track 11

A. Wen-ping is writing an article for a lifestyle magazine. She is talking to people about their work routines. Listen and ⟨circle⟩ the correct information.

Sophie

1. **Sophie**
   a. works late at night
   b. goes to bed before 3 A.M.

2. **Carl**
   a. always works all night
   b. sometimes stays in other countries

3. **Young-woo**
   a. often does more than one show a day
   b. always models in hotels

4. **Amy**
   a. works during the day
   b. often eats out with the players

Young-woo

B. Listen again. Does each person like or dislike their present lifestyle? Check (✓) the correct column.

	Likes	Dislikes
1. Sophie	☐	☐
2. Carl	☐	☐
3. Young-woo	☐	☐
4. Amy	☐	☐

Carl

Amy

4 TUNE IN CD 2 Tracks 12 & 13

A. Listen and notice how people use double questions.

Opening question	+	Focus question
Do you surf the Internet much?	+	*What's your favorite Web site?*
How often do you use your phone?	+	*Do you make a lot of calls?*
What's it like being a flight attendant?	+	*Do you work long hours?*

B. Now match each opening question with its focus question. Then listen and check your answers.

Opening question
1. How do you get to school? ___
2. What do you eat for breakfast? ___
3. What time is your last class? ___
4. How often do you send text messages? ___
5. What do you like to read? ___

Focus question
a. Do you like comic books?
b. Do you send some every day?
c. Do you have a class in the evening?
d. Do you catch a bus?
e. Do you always eat the same thing?

A. What is your lifestyle like? Complete this survey for yourself.

	Me	My partner
1. When is your first class?	_____	_____
2. When do you eat lunch?	_____	_____
3. What do you have for dinner?	_____	_____
4. What do you do in the evenings?	_____	_____
5. What do you do on Saturdays?	_____	_____
6. What time do you go to bed on Saturdays?	_____	_____

B. Write focus questions for the questions in the survey. The first one is done for you.

Opening question	Focus question
1. When is your first class?	_Do you have one at 8:00?_
2. When do you eat lunch?	_____
3. What do you have for dinner?	_____
4. What do you do in the evenings?	_____
5. What do you do on Saturdays?	_____
6. What time do you go to bed on Saturdays?	_____

C. Work with a partner. Take turns asking and answering double questions and complete the survey for your partner. Use this conversation to start but replace the highlighted parts with your own information.

A: *When is your first class? Do you have one at 8:00?*

B: *No, my first class is at 9:00.*

A: *When do you eat lunch? Do you always eat at the same time?*

B: *I usually eat lunch at 1:00.*

A: *What do you have for dinner? Do you always eat the same thing?*

B: *No, not always but I guess I usually have noodles.*

A: . . .

LESSON OBJECTIVES
▸ Understanding descriptions of plans
▸ Identifying descriptions of events
▸ Using the contraction of *going to*

Lesson 2 What are you going to do this weekend?

1 BEFORE YOU LISTEN

Which of these weekend events sound interesting? Circle your two favorite events. Then compare your answers with a partner.

FASHION
Sat 24
Japanese fashion show
Hotel Glam, 12:30 P.M.,
Free entry

DANCE
Sat 24
Ballroom dancing
competition
Bowtie Ballroom,
8:00 P.M., $10

FOOD
Sat 24 & Sun 25
East Asian Food Fair
Market Street, 9:30 A.M.

RETAIL FAIRS
Sat 24 & Sun 25
International
Electronics Fair
Convention Center,
10:00 A.M., $30

SPORTS
Sun 25
Baseball game
Giants vs. Heroes
Skybox Stadium,
1:30 P.M.

ANIMALS & PETS
Sat 24 & Sun 25
Dog show
City Hall,
10:00 A.M., $25

2 LISTEN AND UNDERSTAND 🎧 CD 2 Track 14

A. Office workers are discussing their plans for the weekend. Listen and check (✓) the correct statement.

1. **a.** David has plans for the weekend. ___
   b. Anne is going to have a busy weekend. ___
2. **a.** The dog show ends on Saturday. ___
   b. Tony is going to go away for the weekend. ___
3. **a.** Silvia wants to go to the Electronics Fair. ___
   b. Hye-won is going to have a relaxing weekend. ___

B. Listen again. Circle the correct answer.

1. Who might need a map of the city this weekend? **a.** David   **b.** Anne
2. Who should use sunscreen this weekend?   **a.** Tony   **b.** Mary
3. Who might use a credit card this weekend?   **a.** Silvia   **b.** Hye-won

3 LISTEN AND UNDERSTAND CD 2 Track 15

A. Friends are looking at the newspaper and discussing events in town. Listen and number these events from 1 to 4.

a. food festival ____   **c.** circus ____

b. magic show ____   **d.** table-tennis championship ____

B. Listen again. Circle the correct information.

1. *Both of them are / One of them is* going to go.
2. *One of them / Neither of them is* going to go.
3. *Both of them are / One of them is* going to go.
4. *Both of them are / One of them is* going to go.

4 TUNE IN CD 2 Tracks 16 & 17

A. Listen and notice how people contract *going to* in informal speech so it sounds like *gonna*.

Formal speech	Informal speech
I'm **going to** take them sightseeing on Saturday.	I'm **gonna** take them sightseeing on Saturday.
We're **going to** see a pop concert on Sunday.	We're **gonna** see a pop concert on Sunday.
We're **going to** go to the beach.	We're **gonna** go to the beach.

B. Now listen to phone messages. Is *going to* contracted or not? Check (✓) the correct column.

	going to	*gonna*
1.	☐	☐
2.	☐	☐
3.	☐	☐
4.	☐	☐
5.	☐	☐
6.	☐	☐

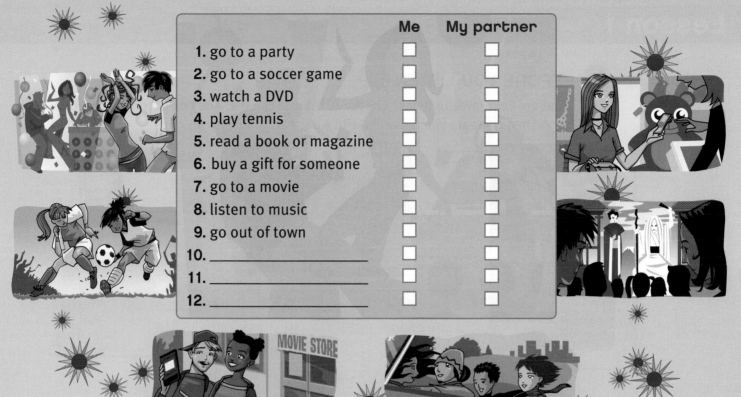

5 AFTER YOU LISTEN

A. What are your plans for this weekend? Complete this survey for yourself. Add three more activities of your own. Check (✓) the activities you are going to do.

	Me	My partner
1. go to a party	☐	☐
2. go to a soccer game	☐	☐
3. watch a DVD	☐	☐
4. play tennis	☐	☐
5. read a book or magazine	☐	☐
6. buy a gift for someone	☐	☐
7. go to a movie	☐	☐
8. listen to music	☐	☐
9. go out of town	☐	☐
10. _____	☐	☐
11. _____	☐	☐
12. _____	☐	☐

B. Work with a partner. Take turns asking and answering questions and complete the survey for your partner. Use this conversation to start but replace the highlighted parts with your own information.

A: *Are you going to go to a party?*
B: *Yes, I'm going to go to a party on Sunday.*
A: *Are you going to go to a soccer game?*
B: *No, I'm not.*
A: *. . .*

C. Think of one activity that you are going to do tonight and make up an activity that you are not going to do. Use this conversation but replace the highlighted parts with your own ideas. Can your partner guess which activity is false?

A: *Tonight I'm going to go to a concert and get my hair cut. So which one is false?*
B: *Oh, I don't think you're going to get your hair cut.*
A: *That's right! / That's wrong!*

8 Possessions

LESSON OBJECTIVES
▸ Understanding descriptions of items
▸ Recognizing features of items
▸ Expressing enthusiasm

Lesson 1 Hey, that's cool!

1 BEFORE YOU LISTEN

What are your favorite items? Check (✓) them in the list. Add two other favorite items you have. Then compare your answers with a partner.

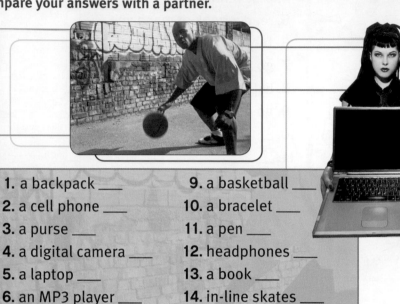

1. a backpack ___
2. a cell phone ___
3. a purse ___
4. a digital camera ___
5. a laptop ___
6. an MP3 player ___
7. a watch ___
8. a skateboard ___

9. a basketball ___
10. a bracelet ___
11. a pen ___
12. headphones ___
13. a book ___
14. in-line skates ___
15. _____
16. _____

2 LISTEN AND UNDERSTAND CD 2 Track 18

A. People are talking about items they own. Listen and number these pictures from 1 to 4.

a. a purse ___   **b.** a pen ___   **c.** a watch ___   **d.** a bracelet ___

B. Listen again. Are these statements true or false? Write *T* (true) or *F* (false).

1. It is made of gold. ___
2. It is pretty and useful. ___
3. It brings him good luck. ___
4. It was a gift from someone. ___

3 LISTEN AND UNDERSTAND 🎧 CD 2 Track 19

A. People are discussing items with sales clerks at an electronics fair. What is the special feature of each item? Listen and check (✓) the correct statement.

1. **a.** The cell phone uses voice dialing. ___
   b. The cell phone weighs less than other phones. ___

2. **a.** The camera folds up to a small size. ___
   b. The camera takes beautiful photos. ___

3. **a.** The MP3 player stores more songs than other MP3 players. ___
   b. The MP3 player works underwater. ___

4. **a.** The TV does not need a screen. ___
   b. The TV's picture is almost as clear as a plasma TV. ___

B. Listen again. Do you think the person will buy the item? Check (✓) the correct column.

	Yes	No
1.	☐	☐
2.	☐	☐
3.	☐	☐
4.	☐	☐

4 TUNE IN CD 2 Tracks 20 & 21

A. Listen and notice how people express enthusiasm about something they see or hear.

> A: *May I show you our new cell phone?*
> B: *Yeah, it looks awesome.*
>
> A: *Let me show you.*
> B: *That's amazing!*
>
> A: *This phone dials for you.*
> B: *Cool!*
>
> A: *Watch this.*
> B: *Wow! That's neat.*

B. Now listen to a conversation. Number the expressions you hear from 1 to 5.

a. Amazing! ___

b. Cool. ___

c. That's neat. ___

d. Wow! ___

e. That's awesome. ___

⑤ AFTER YOU LISTEN

A. Put these sentences in order to make two conversations. The first one is done for you. Then practice the conversations with a partner.

Conversation 1

___ Yes, I do. It's cool. Where did you get it?

_1_ Do you like my watch?

___ Really? It's neat. How much was it?

___ That's awesome.

___ Only $15.00.

___ I bought it at a department store.

Conversation 2

___ You can? That's amazing! Where did you get it?

___ Yeah, it's a Canon. It takes short videos as well as pictures.

___ Yeah, but you can fold it up and make it smaller when you're not using it.

___ That's neat. It's quite big, though.

_1_ Hey, is that a camera?

___ At Camera World downtown. It was half price.

___ But it was probably still quite expensive.

B. Which item in these photos do you like the best? What do you like about it? Work with a partner. Take turns talking about the item you like best. Use this conversation but replace the highlighted parts with features in the box and your own ideas.

has good picture quality	weighs less than others	
uses voice dialing	has a digital camera	has a big screen

A: *Hey, do you like my new* MP3 player *?*

B: *Yes, I do. It's cool.*

A: *And it* has a digital camera, *too!*

B: *That's amazing! Do you use it a lot?*

A: *Yes, it* weighs less than others *so* it's easy to carry around*.*

Lesson 2 What a terrific collection!

1 BEFORE YOU LISTEN

What do you think of these items people collect? Choose a word in the box to describe each collection. Then compare your answers with a partner.

| cool | neat | awesome | cute | weird | ugly | fun | boring | creepy |

1. _____

2. _____

3. _____

4. _____

5. _____

6. _____

2 LISTEN AND UNDERSTAND 🎧 CD 2 Track 22

A. The hosts of a radio show are talking about people's collections. Listen and number these pictures from 1 to 4.

a. banana objects ___   **b.** autographed drumsticks ___   **c.** yo-yos ___   **d.** colored records ___

B. Listen again. Fix the mistakes in these sentences.

1. Peter Lavinger has 300 autographed drumsticks. _____
2. John Meisenheimer keeps his yo-yos in 33 boxes. _____
3. Alessandro Benedetti has 80 records with pictures on them. _____
4. Ken Bannister has 70,000 banana objects. _____

3 LISTEN AND UNDERSTAND 🎧 CD 2 Track 23

A. Young people are calling stores to find items for their collections. Are these statements true or false? Write *T* (true) or *F* (false).

1. The caller is looking for the poster from the third Harry Potter movie. ___
2. The Elvis Presley albums cost $50.00 or more. ___
3. The store has a lot of T-shirts from the 2002 World Cup series. ___

B. Listen again. Will the person buy the item? Check (✓) the correct column.

	Yes	No
1.	☐	☐
2.	☐	☐
3.	☐	☐

4 TUNE IN 🎧 CD 2 Tracks 24 & 25

A. Listen and notice how people check understanding by using echo questions.

> **A:** *Do you have posters from the Harry Potter movies?*
> **B:** ***Harry Potter movie posters?*** *Let me see.*
>
> **A:** *We have all the Lord of the Rings posters.*
> **B:** ***Lord of the Rings?*** *No, I've got those, thanks.*
>
> **A:** *I'm looking for things for my Elvis Presley collection.*
> **B:** ***Elvis Presley things?*** *We have a lot of them.*

B. Now listen to other conversations and circle the echo question you hear.

1. **a.** Old stamps?   **b.** Stamps?
2. **a.** 1950s' stamps?   **b.** Stamps from the 1950s?
3. **a.** China in the 1950s? **b.** Chinese stamps?
4. **a.** Airplanes and taxis? **b.** Trains and factories?

5 AFTER YOU LISTEN

A. Would you like to collect any of these items? Check (✓) at least two items in the list. Add two more items of your own. Answer the follow-up questions about the items you checked.

Items to collect	Follow-up questions	Answers
1. stamps ___	What kind of stamps?	_____
2. toys ___	What kind of toys?	_____
3. posters ___	What kind of posters?	_____
4. CDs ___	What kind of CDs?	_____
5. model cars ___	What kind of cars?	_____
6. dolls ___	What kind of dolls?	_____
7. coins ___	What kind of coins?	_____
8. trading cards ___	What kind of trading cards?	_____
9. _____	What kind of _____?	_____
10. _____	What kind of _____?	_____

B. Work with a partner. Try to guess which items your partner wants to collect. When you guess correctly, ask the follow-up question in part A. Use this conversation to start but replace the highlighted parts with your own information.

A: *Would you like to collect stamps?*

B: *Stamps? Yes, I would.*

A: *What kind of stamps?*

B: *Stamps with sports heroes on them, I think.*

A: *Would you like to collect toys?*

B: *Toys? No, I wouldn't.*

A: *Would you like to collect posters?*

B: *. . .*

LESSON OBJECTIVES
> Identifying parts of the body
> Recognizing descriptions of problems
> Clarifying information

Lesson 1   Where does it hurt?

1 BEFORE YOU LISTEN

Can you find these parts of the body in the pictures? Number them from 1 to 14. Then compare your answers with a partner.

1. leg
2. back
3. arm
4. eye
5. nose
6. head
7. knee
8. foot
9. stomach
10. neck
11. shoulder
12. ankle
13. hand
14. face

2 LISTEN AND UNDERSTAND CD 2 Track 26

A. Young people are describing their injuries to a doctor. Listen and check (✓) the correct part of the body that is hurt.

1. **a.** her knee ___   **b.** her hands ___   **c.** her ear ___
2. **a.** his foot ___   **b.** his shoulders ___   **c.** his eyes ___
3. **a.** his ankle ___   **b.** his arm ___   **c.** his neck ___
4. **a.** her foot ___   **b.** her back ___   **c.** her nose ___

B. Listen again. Are these statements true or false? Write *T* (true) or *F* (false).

1. The patient did not know the pot was hot. ___
2. The patient wore sunscreen all over his body. ___
3. The patient does not use the computer a lot. ___
4. The patient was not wearing shoes when it happened. ___

3 LISTEN AND UNDERSTAND 🎧 CD 2 Track 27

A. People are calling a health clinic for appointments. Listen and check (✓) each person's problem.

1. **a.** a sore knee ___   **b.** a sore arm ___
2. **a.** a backache ___   **b.** an earache ___
3. **a.** an eye infection ___   **b.** a hearing problem ___
4. **a.** a swollen leg ___   **b.** a cut leg ___

B. Listen again. Fix the mistakes in the clinic's appointment schedule.

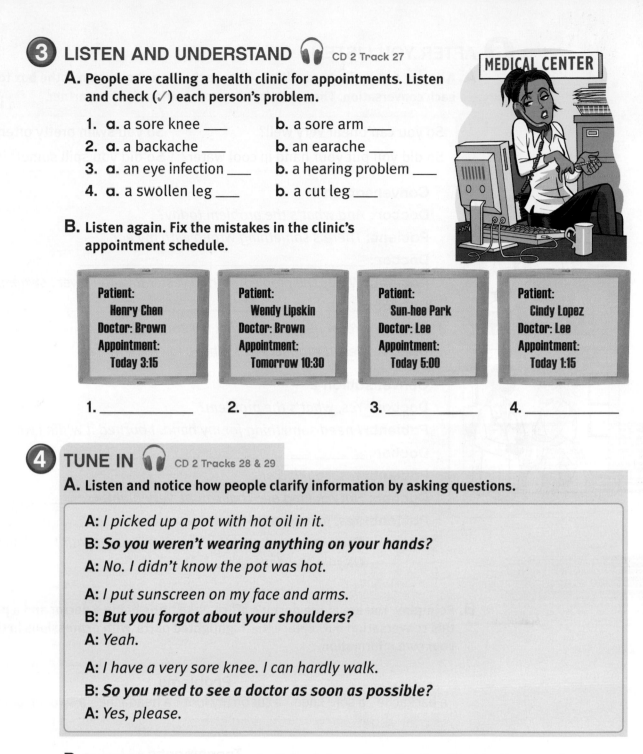

Patient:
Henry Chen
Doctor: Brown
Appointment:
Today 3:15

Patient:
Wendy Lipskin
Doctor: Brown
Appointment:
Tomorrow 10:30

Patient:
Sun-hee Park
Doctor: Lee
Appointment:
Today 5:00

Patient:
Cindy Lopez
Doctor: Lee
Appointment:
Today 1:15

1. _____   2. _____   3. _____   4. _____

4 TUNE IN 🎧 CD 2 Tracks 28 & 29

A. Listen and notice how people clarify information by asking questions.

> **A:** *I picked up a pot with hot oil in it.*
> **B:** ***So you weren't wearing anything on your hands?***
> **A:** *No. I didn't know the pot was hot.*
>
> **A:** *I put sunscreen on my face and arms.*
> **B:** ***But you forgot about your shoulders?***
> **A:** *Yeah.*
>
> **A:** *I have a very sore knee. I can hardly walk.*
> **B:** ***So you need to see a doctor as soon as possible?***
> **A:** *Yes, please.*

B. Now listen to other people clarifying information. Number the questions you hear from 1 to 6.

a. But they didn't help? ___
b. So you haven't been here before? ___
c. So this isn't the first time? ___
d. But you haven't taken anything for it? ___
e. So you were using a knife? ___
f. So you play a lot of tennis, do you? ___

5 AFTER YOU LISTEN

A. A doctor and patient are talking. Choose the correct question in the box to complete each conversation. Then practice the conversations with a partner.

> So you can't hear very well?   So you swim pretty often?
>
> So did you put your hand in cool water?   So did you spill something hot on it?

Conversation 1

Doctor: *And what's the problem today?*

Patient: *There's something wrong with my ear.*

Doctor: _____

Patient: *What? The problem started yesterday after I went swimming.*

Doctor: _____

Patient: *Yes, I do. Do you think my ear's infected?*

Doctor: *Yes, it probably is. I'll have to check it.*

Conversation 2

Doctor: *Yes, what's the problem?*

Patient: *I need something for my hand. I burned it while I was cooking.*

Doctor: _____

Patient: *Yes, cooking oil.*

Doctor: *Hot cooking oil? That can be very painful.* _____

Patient: *Yes, for about 20 minutes.*

Doctor: *That was good. Buy this cream to put on your hand and it'll be OK in a few days.*

B. Role-play. You are at the doctor's office. Take turns being a doctor and a patient. Use this conversation but replace the highlighted parts with expressions in the boxes or your own information.

> ### Problems
> a backache   a sore knee   a cut on my foot   a headache   a swollen ankle   a sunburn

> ### Treatments
> put this cream on it   use a heating pad   take some painkillers
> get some rest   take this medicine   put ice on it

Doctor: *Hello. How can I help you today?*

Patient: *I have a backache.*

Doctor: *Hmm. Let me see. Does this hurt?*

Patient: *Yes!*

Doctor: *I see. Well, you need to use a heating pad and take some painkillers.*

Patient: *OK. Thank you.*

LESSON OBJECTIVES
▸ Understanding instructions
▸ Understanding descriptions of exercises
▸ Giving supporting and contrasting information

Lesson 2 Now try this!

① BEFORE YOU LISTEN

Match each picture with its instruction. Then compare your answers with a partner.

a. b. c. d. e.

1. Hold your leg out in front of you. ___
2. Touch your nose with your finger. ___
3. Put your hands on your head. ___
4. Stand on your right foot. ___
5. Touch your knee with your elbow. ___

② LISTEN AND UNDERSTAND 🎧 CD 2 Track 30

A. A teacher is giving instructions to an exercise class. Listen and number these pictures from 1 to 6.

a. ___ b. ___ c. ___ d. ___ e. ___ f. ___

B. Listen again. Was the teacher happy or unhappy with how the class followed the instructions? Check (✓) the correct column.

	Happy	Unhappy
1.	☐	☐
2.	☐	☐
3.	☐	☐
4.	☐	☐
5.	☐	☐
6.	☐	☐

LISTEN AND UNDERSTAND 🎧 CD 2 Track 31

A. People are describing things they do for relaxation and exercise. Listen and number these activities from 1 to 5.

    a. power walking ___

    b. aerobics ___

    c. meditation ___

    d. line dancing ___

    e. tai chi ___

B. Listen again. What do people say about their activities? Circle the correct answer.

    1. a. Alex does it once a week.   **b.** Alex sometimes falls asleep.

    2. a. It is really hard work.   **b.** Nicholas does it at home.

    3. a. The group dances to rock music.   **b.** The group wears cowboy hats and boots.

    4. a. Katy does it every day.   **b.** The music is very relaxing.

    5. a. You run very fast.   **b.** You move your arms up and down.

4 **TUNE IN** 🎧 CD 2 Tracks 32 & 33

A. Listen and notice how people give supporting and contrasting information about an idea.

Supporting information	Contrasting information
Meditation helps me relax. ***And what's more,*** *I enjoy it.*	*Our aerobics class is really hard work.* ***On the other hand,*** *you feel great when you're done.*
Tai chi is very slow and gentle. ***And another thing,*** *the Chinese music we play is very relaxing.*	*Tai chi is very slow and gentle.* ***And yet*** *it really stretches your muscles.*
You move very fast, but you don't run. *You* ***also*** *move your arms up and down.*	*Line dancing is a lot of fun.* ***However,*** *you do have to love the music.*

B. Now listen to other conversations. Does the second person give supporting or contrasting information in each conversation? Check (✓) the correct column.

	Supporting information	Contrasting information
1.	☐	☐
2.	☐	☐
3.	☐	☐
4.	☐	☐
5.	☐	☐
6.	☐	☐

5 AFTER YOU LISTEN

A. Work with a partner. Match each of these statements with two sentences in the box: one with supporting information and one with contrasting information. The first one is done for you.

	Supporting	Contrasting
1. Swimming is a great sport.	b	g
2. Skateboarding is an exciting sport to watch live.	___	___
3. You do not need to be very fit to enjoy line dancing.	___	___
4. Power walking is a good way to keep fit.	___	___

> **a.** However, it can be boring.
>
> **b.** And also it keeps you cool in the summer.
>
> **c.** And another thing, it's a good way to meet people.
>
> **d.** And also, it is a sport that older people can enjoy.
>
> **e.** And also a fun sport to try yourself.
>
> **f.** However, it often leads to serious injuries.
>
> **g.** On the other hand, you can get ear infections from the water.
>
> **h.** However, you do need to be a pretty good dancer.

B. Work with a partner. Complete these statements with the names of sports.

Statements	Supporting or contrasting information
1. _____ is a great sport.	_____
2. _____ is a good way to keep fit.	_____

C. Individually, write supporting or contrasting information for the statements in part B. Then compare your answers with your partner. Did you add the same or different information?

Clothes & Fashion

Lesson 1   I like your shirt!

1 BEFORE YOU LISTEN

A. Where would you wear these clothes? Check (✓) one or more columns for each item. Then compare your answers with a partner.

	To school	To work	To a party	Nowhere
1. a jacket	☐	☐	☐	☐
2. sneakers	☐	☐	☐	☐
3. jeans	☐	☐	☐	☐
4. shorts	☐	☐	☐	☐
5. a tie	☐	☐	☐	☐
6. a suit	☐	☐	☐	☐
7. pants	☐	☐	☐	☐
8. a sweater	☐	☐	☐	☐
9. a shirt	☐	☐	☐	☐
10. sandals	☐	☐	☐	☐

B. What clothes are you wearing today? Ask and answer with a partner.

2 LISTEN AND UNDERSTAND 🎧 CD 2 Track 34

A. People are packing for a trip. Listen and circle the items each person will take. More than one answer is possible.

1. **a.** sandals **b.** boots **c.** jacket **d.** swimming trunks
2. **a.** shirts **b.** ties **c.** T-shirts **d.** umbrella
3. **a.** sweaters **b.** coat **c.** pants **d.** shorts
4. **a.** jeans **b.** jacket **c.** sandals **d.** boots

B. Listen again. Where is each person going? Check (✓) the correct answer.

1. **a.** beach vacation ___ **b.** business trip ___ **c.** ski trip ___
2. **a.** beach vacation ___ **b.** business trip ___ **c.** camping trip ___
3. **a.** beach vacation ___ **b.** business trip ___ **c.** ski trip ___
4. **a.** beach vacation ___ **b.** business trip ___ **c.** camping trip ___

3 LISTEN AND UNDERSTAND 🎧 CD 2 Track 35

A. A TV reporter is interviewing people on the street about how they dress for work. Listen and number these pictures from 1 to 4.

a. ___   b. ___   c. ___   d. ___

B. Listen again. Check (✓) the correct statement.

1. The teacher
- **a.** dresses formally for work. ___
- **b.** always wears comfortable shoes. ___

2. The receptionist
- **a.** does not spend money on work clothes. ___
- **b.** does not like his uniform. ___

3. The banker
- **a.** wears a suit to work. ___
- **b.** likes the dress code at work. ___

4. The office worker
- **a.** wears a tie to work. ___
- **b.** likes to dress casually. ___

4 TUNE IN 🎧 CD 2 Tracks 36 & 37

A. Listen and notice how people express uncertainty when they are not sure about an answer or do not want to say yes or no directly.

> **Uncertainty or *yes***
>
> **A:** *Should I take a hat?*
> - **B:** *I think so.*
> - **B:** *I suppose so.*
> - **B:** *I guess so.*
>
> **Uncertainty or *no***
>
> **A:** *Do you think uniforms are boring?*
> - **B:** *No, I don't think so.*
> - **B:** *Not really.*

B. Now listen to other conversations. Does the answer to each question mean *yes* or *no*? Check (✓) the correct column.

	Yes	No			Yes	No			Yes	No
1.	☐	☐		3.	☐	☐		5.	☐	☐
2.	☐	☐		4.	☐	☐		6.	☐	☐

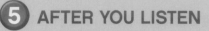
A. What do you think of clothes and fashion? Complete this survey for yourself. Circle *yes* or *no*. Think of reasons for three of your answers.

Do you think. . .	Me		My partner	
1. college students should wear uniforms?	Yes	No	Yes	No
2. earrings look good on men?	Yes	No	Yes	No
3. tattoos look good on people?	Yes	No	Yes	No
4. people should be able to wear jeans to work?	Yes	No	Yes	No
5. it is OK for men to color their hair?	Yes	No	Yes	No
6. designer clothes are better than other brands?	Yes	No	Yes	No
7. women are more interested in clothes than men?	Yes	No	Yes	No
8. it is important to wear the latest fashions?	Yes	No	Yes	No

B. Work with a partner. Take turns asking and answering questions and complete the survey for your partner. Use this conversation but replace the highlighted parts with expressions in the box and your own reasons.

I guess so.   I think so.   I suppose so.   No, I don't think so.   No, not really.

A: *Do you think college students should wear uniforms?*
B: *I think so. I think they look fashionable.*
A: *Do you think earrings look good on men?*
B: *No, not really. To me they look silly.*

LESSON OBJECTIVES
▸ Identifying features of clothes
▸ Understanding information about people
▸ Expressing agreement or disagreement

Lesson 2   Where did you buy those jeans?

1 BEFORE YOU LISTEN

What is important to you when you buy clothes? Rank this list from 1 (most important) to 6 (least important). Then compare your answers with a partner.

___ price

___ style

___ brand

___ quality

___ comfort

___ fashion

2 LISTEN AND UNDERSTAND CD 2 Track 38

A. People are talking about clothes in a store. Listen and circle the feature they discuss.

1. **a.** comfort   **b.** quality
2. **a.** quality   **b.** style
3. **a.** brand   **b.** color
4. **a.** comfort   **b.** style
5. **a.** style   **b.** brand

B. Listen again. Write the price of each item. Will the person buy it or not? Check (✓) the correct column.

Item	Price	Will buy	Will not buy
1. shirt	_____	☐	☐
2. jeans	_____	☐	☐
3. sneakers	_____	☐	☐
4. tie	_____	☐	☐
5. earrings	_____	☐	☐

3 LISTEN AND UNDERSTAND 🎧 CD 2 Track 39

A. College friends are talking about how they like to dress. Does the second person have the same or a different opinion? Listen and check (✓) the correct column.

	Same	Different
1.	☐	☐
2.	☐	☐
3.	☐	☐
4.	☐	☐
5.	☐	☐

B. Listen again. Are these statements true or false? Write *T* (true) or *F* (false).

1. Sally often buys second-hand clothes. ___
2. Pei-ting hates to be noticed. ___
3. Kevin and Linda usually buy designer clothes. ___
4. Jack likes to wear comfortable clothes. ___
5. Ben hardly ever dresses up. ___

4 TUNE IN 🎧 CD 2 Tracks 40 & 41

A. Listen and notice how people express agreement and disagreement with opinions.

Agreement

A: *This shirt looks very well made.*

B: *I think you're right.*

A: *The price is reasonable, too.*

B: *I agree.*

Disagreement

A: *It's fun to wear bright colors.*

B: *Really? Do you think so? I like to wear soft, warm colors.*

A: *It doesn't matter what clothes look like if they're comfortable.*

B: *I don't know about that. I think style is important.*

B. Now listen to people giving their opinions. Does the second person express agreement or disagreement with the opinion in each conversation? Circle the correct answer.

1. **a.** agreement   **b.** disagreement   4. **a.** agreement   **b.** disagreement
2. **a.** agreement   **b.** disagreement   5. **a.** agreement   **b.** disagreement
3. **a.** agreement   **b.** disagreement   6. **a.** agreement   **b.** disagreement

5 AFTER YOU LISTEN

A. Match each statement with its response. Then practice the conversations with a partner.

1. It's important to be fashionable. ___
2. It's fine to wear shorts to a wedding. ___
3. Dark clothes look more fashionable. ___
4. You should wear a suit to work. ___
5. Designer clothes are the best. ___

a. Do you think so? I think white clothes are more fashionable.
b. I think you're right, but they're expensive.
c. Maybe, but I think pants are better.
d. I'm not sure. It depends on your job.
e. I don't know about that. I like being comfortable.

B. What do you like to wear? Complete this survey for yourself. Add two more questions of your own and answer them.

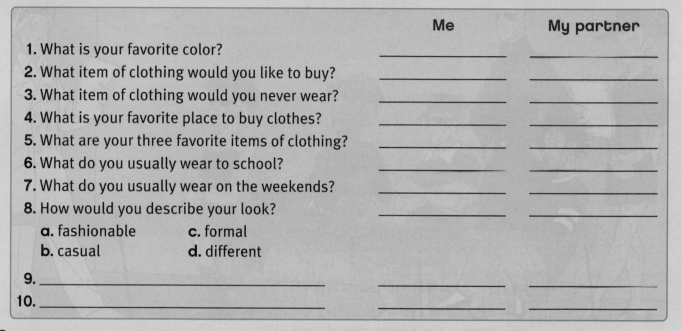

	Me	My partner
1. What is your favorite color?	_____	_____
2. What item of clothing would you like to buy?	_____	_____
3. What item of clothing would you never wear?	_____	_____
4. What is your favorite place to buy clothes?	_____	_____
5. What are your three favorite items of clothing?	_____	_____
6. What do you usually wear to school?	_____	_____
7. What do you usually wear on the weekends?	_____	_____
8. How would you describe your look?	_____	_____

    a. fashionable   c. formal
    b. casual   d. different

9. _____   _____   _____
10. _____   _____   _____

C. Work with a partner. Take turns asking and answering the questions and complete the survey for your partner. Do you and your partner have the same look?

LESSON OBJECTIVES
▸ Recognizing descriptions of instruments
▸ Identifying information about people
▸ Showing you are listening

Lesson 1 He's a great drummer!

1 BEFORE YOU LISTEN

Do you play any of these musical instruments? Which ones would you like to learn?
Check (✓) the correct column. Then compare your answers with a partner.

	I can play	I would like to learn
1. the piano	☐	☐
2. the violin	☐	☐
3. the drums	☐	☐
4. the guitar	☐	☐
5. the flute	☐	☐
6. the saxophone	☐	☐
7. the trumpet	☐	☐
8. the clarinet	☐	☐

2 LISTEN AND UNDERSTAND 🎧 CD 3 Track 02

A. A music store clerk is talking to customers about musical instruments. Listen and
number these instruments from 1 to 5.

a. a trumpet ___   c. a guitar ___   e. a violin ___
b. drums ___   d. a piano ___

B. Listen again. What will each person say next? Check (✓) the best answer.

1. a. Well, I'm sure he'll enjoy that. ___
   b. Oh, I'm sorry to hear that. ___

2. a. That's a good way to learn. ___
   b. Oh, I'll tell her to be careful. ___

3. a. Do you know a good teacher? ___
   b. So I guess it's better to teach yourself. ___

4. a. Oh, we have a big family. ___
   b. Sure, she can practice in the basement. ___

5. a. Too bad. He really wanted to start playing. ___
   b. Great. And do you give piano lessons here? ___

A. A radio announcer is talking about musicians. Listen and check (✓) the correct statement.

1. **a.** Alicia Keys began writing songs when she was a teenager. ___
   b. Alicia Keys graduated from Columbia University. ___
2. **a.** Vanessa-Mae was born in London. ___
   b. Vanessa-Mae had recorded three albums by the age of 13. ___
3. **a.** Lang Lang gave his first concert when he was five years old. ___
   b. Lang Lang played with the Chicago Symphony Orchestra at the age of seven. ___

B. Listen again. Complete the chart with the correct information.

	Alicia Keys	Vanessa-Mae	Lang Lang
Born (year)			1982
Born (country)	US		
First music lessons (age)		5	

 TUNE IN 🎧 CD 3 Tracks 04 & 05

A. Listen and notice how people show they are listening.

A: *Drums make a lot of noise.*	B: *That's for sure.* B: *I know.*
A: *It's important to hold the violin correctly.*	B: *Uh-huh.* B: *That's right.* B: *That's true.*

B. Now listen to a conversation. Check (✓) these expressions each time you hear them.

1. That's for sure.   ___ ___ ___ ___ ___
2. I know.   ___ ___ ___ ___ ___
3. Uh-huh.   ___ ___ ___ ___ ___
4. That's right.   ___ ___ ___ ___ ___
5. That's true.   ___ ___ ___ ___ ___

5 AFTER YOU LISTEN

A. What kind of music do you like? Complete this survey for yourself. Add two more questions of your own and answer them.

	Me	Student A	Student B
1. What kind of music do you like?	_____	_____	_____
2. What kind of music do you dislike?	_____	_____	_____
3. Who is your favorite male singer?	_____	_____	_____
4. Who is your favorite female singer?	_____	_____	_____
5. What is your favorite music group?	_____	_____	_____
6. Which music show(s) do you watch on TV?	_____	_____	_____
7. Which radio station(s) do you listen to?	_____	_____	_____
8. What music performances do you attend?	_____	_____	_____
9. Do you have an MP3 player?	_____	_____	_____
10. How many CDs do you have?	_____	_____	_____
11. _____	_____	_____	_____
12. _____	_____	_____	_____

B. Work with two classmates. Take turns asking and answering the questions and complete the survey for your classmates. Use this conversation to start but replace the highlighted parts with your own information. Which questions did all three of you answer in the same way?

A: *What kind of music do you like?*

B: *I like* R&B and hip hop.

A: *What kind of music do you dislike?*

B: *I dislike* classical music.

A: *Who is your favorite male singer?*

B: *I really like* Usher.

A: *Who is your favorite female singer?*

B: *I really like* BoA.

A: *What is your favorite group?*

B: *I don't really have a favorite group.*

A: . . .

LESSON OBJECTIVES
▸ Understanding information about events
▸ Recognizing people's intentions
▸ Accepting and declining invitations

Lesson 2 How was the concert?

1 BEFORE YOU LISTEN

Have you ever been to these events? Did you like them or not? Check (✓) the correct columns. Then compare your answers with a partner.

	Yes	No	I liked it.	I did not like it.
1. a rock concert	☐	☐	☐	☐
2. a musical	☐	☐	☐	☐
3. a ballet	☐	☐	☐	☐
4. a symphony concert	☐	☐	☐	☐
5. a piano recital	☐	☐	☐	☐
6. a pop concert	☐	☐	☐	☐
7. an opera	☐	☐	☐	☐

2 LISTEN AND UNDERSTAND 🎧 CD 3 Track 06

A. A radio announcer is giving information about musical events. Does he say *when* or *where* the events will take place? Listen and check (✓) the correct column.

	When	Where
1.	☐	☐
2.	☐	☐
3.	☐	☐
4.	☐	☐

B. Listen again. What other information does the announcer give? Circle the two things he says about each event.

1. **a.** price   **b.** seating   **c.** tickets
2. **a.** seating   **b.** price   **c.** weather
3. **a.** performer   **b.** program   **c.** clothing
4. **a.** price   **b.** length of show   **c.** food

3 LISTEN AND UNDERSTAND CD 3 Track 07

A. Friends are talking about events in town. Listen and check (✓) the correct statement.

1. **a.** The Five Stars have been famous for years. ___
   b. Both friends have heard of the group. ___

2. **a.** The Rain concert is next week. ___
   b. Both friends would like to see him. ___

3. **a.** Kayla is a professional guitar player. ___
   b. The tickets are only $10.00. ___

4. **a.** The TV show is a singing competition. ___
   b. Su-wei is going to buy two tickets. ___

B. Listen again. Will both people go to the event? Check (✓) the correct column.

	Yes	No
1.	☐	☐
2.	☐	☐
3.	☐	☐
4.	☐	☐

4 TUNE IN 🎧 CD 3 Tracks 08 & 09

A. Listen and notice how people accept and decline invitations.

Invitations	Accept
A: *Are you interested in going to a rock concert?*	B: *That sounds great.*
	B: *Sure, I'd love to.*
	B: *Thanks, that sounds nice.*
	Decline
A: *Would you like to go to the Pop Idol show?*	B: *I'm afraid I can't.*
	B: *Sorry, I can't.*
	B: *I'd love to, but I'm busy tonight.*
	B: *Thanks, but I don't really like that show.*

B. Now listen to other conversations. Does the second person accept or decline the invitation in each conversation? Circle the correct answer.

1. **a.** accepts   **b.** declines
2. **a.** accepts   **b.** declines
3. **a.** accepts   **b.** declines
4. **a.** accepts   **b.** declines
5. **a.** accepts   **b.** declines

5 AFTER YOU LISTEN

A. Put these sentences in order to make a conversation. The first one is done for you. Then practice the conversation with a partner.

___ *Maybe. What's on?*

___ *See you.*

___ *There's a musical called* Stage Lights *at the Capital Theater. I hear it's very good.*

___ *That sounds interesting. Yeah, I'd love to go.*

_1_ *Would you like to see a show Saturday night?*

___ *Great. I'll get tickets. What time do you want to meet? The show starts at 8 o'clock.*

___ *OK. See you Saturday.*

___ *Why don't we meet in front of the theater at 7:30?*

B. Work with a partner. Circle the two events you would like to attend. Take turns inviting each other to one of the events. Accept the invitation if you circled the event or decline if you did not. Use this conversation but replace the highlighted parts with information in the posters and your own ideas.

A: *Would you like to go to a* rock concert *this weekend?*

B: *Sure. That sounds interesting. When is it?*

A: *It's* Friday at 8 o'clock.

B: *And where is it?*

A: *It's at the* National Stadium.

B: *Great. I'd love to go. What time shall we meet?*

A: *Let's meet at* 7 o'clock *in front of the subway station.*

B: *Would you like to go to a* piano recital *on* Saturday?

A: *Thanks, that sounds nice. What time is it?*

B: *It's at* 7 o'clock.

A: *Oh, I'm afraid I can't. I'm busy at* 7.

B: *That's too bad.*

Unit
12 Food

LESSON OBJECTIVES
▸ Understanding offers and replies
▸ Identifying descriptions of meals
▸ Using short forms of questions

Lesson 1   Would you care for a snack?

1 BEFORE YOU LISTEN

A. How often do you eat these snacks? Check (✓) the correct column. Then compare your answers with a partner.

	Often	Sometimes	Never
1. chocolates	☐	☐	☐
2. fruit	☐	☐	☐
3. popcorn	☐	☐	☐
4. French fries	☐	☐	☐
5. ice cream	☐	☐	☐
6. potato chips	☐	☐	☐

B. Write your three favorite snacks. Then compare your answers with a partner.

1. _____ 2. _____ 3. _____

2 LISTEN AND UNDERSTAND CD 3 Track 10

A. People are offering snacks to their friends. Does the second person accept or decline? Listen and check (✓) the correct column.

	Accepts	Declines			Accepts	Declines
1.	☐	☐		4.	☐	☐
2.	☐	☐		5.	☐	☐
3.	☐	☐		6.	☐	☐

B. Listen again. What do you think the friends will do next? Check (✓) the correct answer.

1. **a.** play a video game ___   **b.** play tennis ___
2. **a.** watch a DVD ___   **b.** listen to music ___
3. **a.** go to a movie ___   **b.** go swimming ___
4. **a.** keep watching the TV show ___   **b.** watch a different TV show ___
5. **a.** look at the new computer ___   **b.** look at a magazine ___
6. **a.** keep playing chess ___   **b.** play basketball ___

3 LISTEN AND UNDERSTAND 🎧 CD 3 Track 11

A. People are talking about what they eat for lunch. Listen and number these pictures from 1 to 6.

a. ___ b. ___ c. ___ d. ___ e. ___ f. ___

B. Listen again. What reasons do people give for their lunch choices? Circle the correct answer.

1. Ken's lunch is *cheap / healthy*.
2. Emi is *not very hungry / not very busy* at lunchtime.
3. The man and woman do not have enough *time / money* to eat a big lunch.
4. Maria thinks rice and bread are *healthy / fattening*.
5. Jeff likes to eat a *cold / hot* lunch.
6. Claire and Terry think sushi is *easy / delicious*.

4 TUNE IN 🎧 CD 3 Tracks 12 & 13

A. Listen and notice how people use short forms of questions in informal speech.

Full question	Short form
*Do you **want something to eat**?*	***Want something to eat?***
*Would you **care to try one**?*	***Care to try one?***
*Would you **like a snack**?*	***Like a snack?***
*Do you **mind if I join you**?*	***Mind if I join you?***

B. Now listen to short conversations. Do you hear a full question or a short form of question in each conversation? Check (✓) the correct column.

	Full question	Short form
1.	☐	☐
2.	☐	☐
3.	☐	☐
4.	☐	☐
5.	☐	☐
6.	☐	☐

5 AFTER YOU LISTEN

A. Role-play. Your friend is going to pick up some snacks. What would you like to eat and drink? Check (✓) three items on this order form.

cookies ☐

popcorn ☐   soda ☐

nuts ☐   tea ☐

fruit ☐   coffee ☐

chocolates ☐   milk ☐

ice cream ☐   juice ☐

potato chips ☐   water ☐

cheese ☐

B. Work with a partner. Take turns offering to get snacks for each other. Use this conversation but replace the highlighted parts with items in part A or your own ideas.

A: *I'm going out to get something to eat. Care for anything?*

B: *Yeah, could you pick up a snack for me?*

A: *Sure. What would you like?*

B: *Could you get me some cookies?*

A: *OK. And do you want anything to drink?*

B: *Yes, I'd like some coffee.*

A: *Sure. No problem.*

Lesson 2   What are we having for dinner?

1 BEFORE YOU LISTEN

Match the ingredients with these British, Italian, and Asian rice dishes. Which dish would you like to try? Compare your answers with a partner.

1. rice pudding ___   **2.** mushroom risotto ___   **3.** shrimp fried rice ___

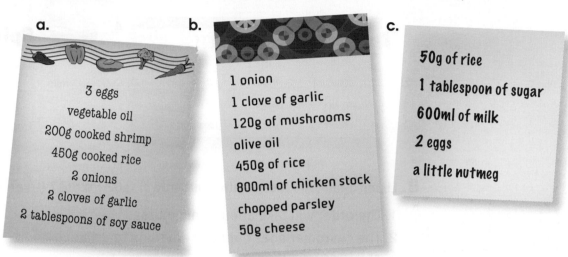

a.

3 eggs
vegetable oil
200g cooked shrimp
450g cooked rice
2 onions
2 cloves of garlic
2 tablespoons of soy sauce

b.

1 onion
1 clove of garlic
120g of mushrooms
olive oil
450g of rice
800ml of chicken stock
chopped parsley
50g cheese

c.

50g of rice
1 tablespoon of sugar
600ml of milk
2 eggs
a little nutmeg

2 LISTEN AND UNDERSTAND 🎧 CD 3 Track 14

A. A chef is making rice on a TV cooking show. Which dishes is the chef making? Listen and check (✓) the correct dish.

1. **a.** mushroom risotto ___   **b.** rice pudding ___   **c.** shrimp fried rice ___
2. **a.** mushroom risotto ___   **b.** rice pudding ___   **c.** shrimp fried rice ___

B. Listen again. Put these instructions in order. The first one is done for you.

1. ___ Stir slowly until all the liquid has disappeared.
   ___ Stir in the rice.
   _1_ Chop the onions and garlic into small pieces.
   ___ Stir in some cheese and then serve.
   ___ Add the stock and some chopped parsley.
   ___ Fry them in olive oil with 120g of mushrooms.

2. ___ Heat some oil and make a thin omelet.
   ___ Fry the shrimp for two to three minutes.
   ___ Beat three eggs with salt and pepper.
   ___ Add the onion and garlic and cook for one to two minutes.
   ___ Remove your pan from the heat and stir in the cooked omelet.
   ___ Stir in the rice and soy sauce.
   ___ Let the omelet cool and then chop it up.

3 LISTEN AND UNDERSTAND 🎧 CD 3 Track 15

A. People are ordering food by telephone. What do they order? Listen and check (✓) the correct information.

1.
Pizza to Go

PIZZA

☐ seafood ☐ mushroom ☐ sausage
☐ small ☐ medium ☐ large
☐ thin crust ☐ thick crust

3.
Burger
☐ cheese ☐ bacon ☐ chili
Fries
☐ small ☐ medium ☐ large
Soda
☐ orange ☐ lemon-lime ☐ grape

Best Burger

2.
ASIAN EXPRESS

RICE

☐ steamed ☐ fried ☐ sticky
☐ small ☐ large
☐ chicken ☐ pork ☐ seafood

4.
Spicy Eats

CHILI CON CARNE
☐ mild ☐ medium ☐ spicy

SALAD
☐ regular ☐ large

B. Listen again. Are these statements true or false? Write *T* (true) or *F* (false).

1. The order will take about ten minutes. ___

2. The customer does not need anything to drink. ___

3. The customer does not want salt on the fries. ___

4. The customer will pick up the order. ___

4 TUNE IN 🎧 CD 3 Tracks 16 & 17

A. Listen and notice how people check understanding by repeating key words.

> **A:** *I'd like a mushroom pizza, please.*
> **B:** ***Mushroom.*** *OK.*
>
> **A:** *I'd like some chili con carne. But I don't want it too spicy.*
> **B:** ***Chili con carne. Not too spicy.*** *Is medium all right?*

B. Now circle the key words in each sentence that you think the second person will repeat. Then listen and check your answers.

1. I'd like two chicken sandwiches. I'm really hungry today.

2. Could you deliver the food before 7:00? I have to leave after that.

3. I think we should have beef kebabs at the barbecue. What do you think?

4. We have two kinds of ice cream. Would you like chocolate or vanilla?

5. When you go to Bangkok, you must try the shrimp soup. It's quite spicy, but it's delicious.

A. What food do you like? Complete the survey for yourself. Add two more questions of your own and answer them.

	Me	My partner
What is your favorite. . .?		
1. meal of the day	_____	_____
a. breakfast		
b. lunch		
c. dinner		
2. home-cooked dinner	_____	_____
3. dessert	_____	_____
4. breakfast food	_____	_____
5. food from another country	_____	_____
6. pizza topping	_____	_____
7. fast-food restaurant	_____	_____
8. fast-food meal	_____	_____
9. _____	_____	_____
10. _____	_____	_____

B. Work with a partner. Take turns asking and answering the questions and complete the survey for your partner. Use this conversation to start but replace the highlighted parts with your own information.

A: *What's your favorite meal of the day?*

B: *I guess it's* lunch.

A: *Lunch. Really? And what's your favorite home-cooked dinner?*

B: *Steak and salad, I'd say.*

A: *Steak and salad. Right. And what's your favorite dessert?*

B: *Well, let me think . . .*

Lesson 1 Where do you live?

1 BEFORE YOU LISTEN

A. What is important to you when choosing a place to live? Rank this list from 1 (most important) to 6 (least important). Then compare your answers with a partner.

___ close to school or work

___ not too expensive

___ not too noisy

___ close to transportation

___ size of room or apartment

___ close to stores and restaurants

B. Where would you prefer to live? Circle your answer. Then compare with a partner.

1. in an apartment with other students
2. in a residence hall
3. with a local family
4. in an apartment by yourself

2 LISTEN AND UNDERSTAND CD 3 Track 18

A. Students are describing their housing preferences. Listen and check (✓) the best option for each student.

1. **a.** stay with a local family ___   **b.** rent an apartment by herself ___
2. **a.** live in a residence hall on campus ___   **b.** rent an apartment downtown ___
3. **a.** rent a house with other students ___   **b.** live in a residence hall on campus ___
4. **a.** stay with a local family ___   **b.** rent an apartment by himself ___

B. Listen again. What will each person say next? Circle the best answer.

1. **a.** What time is the movie?   **b.** That's a good idea.
2. **a.** That's a good idea.   **b.** Maybe you can live in a residence hall.
3. **a.** How many are in the group?   **b.** Is the bus comfortable?
4. **a.** That could be quite expensive.   **b.** Why do you want to buy a house?

3 LISTEN AND UNDERSTAND  CD 3 Track 19

A. College students are talking to a college counselor about their housing. Do they like it or not? Listen and check (✓) the correct column.

Jun-hao

Sam

Emma

Mei-ling

John

	Yes	No
1.	☐	☐
2.	☐	☐
3.	☐	☐
4.	☐	☐
5.	☐	☐

B. Listen again. Are these statements true or false? Write *T* (true) or *F* (false).

1. Jun-hao's room faces the street. ___
2. Sam has to share a bedroom. ___
3. It takes Emma a long time to get to class. ___
4. Mei-ling lives close to campus. ___
5. John's apartment is very comfortable. ___

4 TUNE IN CD 3 Tracks 20 & 21

A. Listen and notice how people express uncertainty when they are not sure about an answer.

> **A:** *Are you going to stay in the same apartment next year?*
>
> **B:** *It depends.*
> **B:** *I'm not sure.*
> **B:** *I don't know.*
> **B:** *Maybe.*

B. Now listen to other people answering questions. Is the second person sure about the answer in each conversation? Check (✓) the correct column.

	Sure	Not sure
1.	☐	☐
2.	☐	☐
3.	☐	☐
4.	☐	☐
5.	☐	☐
6.	☐	☐

A. Look at these advertisements for student housing. Complete the missing information with the numbers in the box. Do not show anyone what you have written.

| 1 | 2 | 3 | 5 | 6 | 10 | 15 | 30 | $100 | $150 | $300 | $500 |

HOME STAY: Room available for student. Family with _____ children. Downtown. _____ minutes from campus, _____ minutes from bus station. Own bathroom. No cooking facilities. Breakfast and dinner included. Rent: _____ a month.

ROOMMATE NEEDED: Share 3-bedroom apartment with _____ other students. _____ minutes from campus, _____ minutes from downtown. Own bedroom. Share kitchen and bathroom. Rent: _____ a month.

RESIDENCE HALL: On campus. _____ students per room. Cafeteria available. Limited cooking facilities. Share bathroom. _____ minutes from library, _____ minutes from gym, pool. Rent: _____ a month.

B. Role-play. You are at a school housing office. Work with a partner. Take turns being a housing officer and a student looking for housing. Use this conversation but replace the highlighted parts with information from the advertisements in part A.

A: *I'm looking for a place to live. What kind of housing is available?*

B: *Well, would you like to live on campus or off campus?*

A: *Off campus, I think.*

B: *OK. And would you like to live with a family or share an apartment?*

A: *Hmm. Share an apartment, I guess.*

B: *Here's something: a 3-bedroom apartment to share with three other students.*

A: *Where is it?*

B: *Fifteen minutes from campus.*

A: *How much is the rent?*

B: *$150 a month. You share the kitchen and bathroom.*

A: *Hmm. Maybe I should look at it.*

LESSON OBJECTIVES
> Understanding ideas and wishes
> Identifying changes and suggestions
> Making and responding to suggestions

Lesson 2 How do you like my room?

① BEFORE YOU LISTEN

Someone has redecorated this room. What changes do you see? Talk about them with a partner. Use the words in the boxes.

| a sofa   armchairs   a TV   a rug   carpeting   curtains   the floor   a stereo |

| darker   lighter   older   more modern |

② LISTEN AND UNDERSTAND CD 3 Track 22

A. Teenagers are talking with their parents about changing things at home. What changes do they want to make? Listen and check (✓) the correct answer.

1. **a.** paint the walls a darker color ___   **b.** paint the walls a lighter color ___
2. **a.** buy a new sofa ___   **b.** buy a new chair ___
3. **a.** get a piano ___   **b.** get a plasma TV ___
4. **a.** get carpeting for the floor ___   **b.** get new tiles for the floor ___

B. Listen again. Does each parent accept or reject the suggestions? Circle the correct answer.

1. **a.** accepts   **b.** rejects
2. **a.** accepts   **b.** rejects
3. **a.** accepts   **b.** rejects
4. **a.** accepts   **b.** rejects

3 LISTEN AND UNDERSTAND 🎧 CD 3 Track 23

A. An interior designer is suggesting changes to people's homes. Are these statements true or false? Write *T* (true) or *F* (false).

1. Use dark colors on the walls and floor. ___
2. Take out a lot of the furniture. ___
3. Try fresh colors and modern furniture. ___
4. Move the window. ___

B. Listen again. How will the changes improve the room? Circle the correct answer.

1. The room will feel *warmer / bigger*.
2. The room will seem *colder / less crowded*.
3. The room will look more *comfortable / modern*.
4. The room will be easier to *clean / get in and out of*.

4 TUNE IN 🎧 CD 3 Tracks 24 & 25

A. Listen and notice how people make and respond to suggestions.

Suggestions	Accept	Reject
Let's try a lighter color.	*All right.*	*I don't think we need to.*
I think we should get a new sofa.	*Yeah, why not?*	*Maybe not.*
Don't you think we should get a new TV?	*That's a good idea.*	*No, I don't think so.*
Why don't we get new carpeting?	*Sure. OK.*	*I don't think we should.*

B. Now listen to people making suggestions. Does the second person accept or reject the suggestion in each conversation? Check (✓) the correct column.

	Accepts	Rejects
1.	☐	☐
2.	☐	☐
3.	☐	☐
4.	☐	☐
5.	☐	☐
6.	☐	☐

AFTER YOU LISTEN

A. Work with a partner. You must give this room a different look but you can only change five things. What would you change? Complete these sentences and give a reason for each change.

Change	Reason
1. Let's fix _____.	_____
2. Let's paint _____.	_____
3. Let's buy _____.	_____
4. Let's add _____.	_____
5. Let's remove _____.	_____

B. Work with another partner. Take turns explaining your changes. Use this conversation but replace the highlighted parts with your own information. How many of your changes are the same? How many are different?

A: *We're going to fix the curtains because they're falling down.*

B: *That's a good idea. Are you going to paint anything?*

A: *Yes. We're going to paint the walls a light color to make the room look bigger.*

B: *I see. Are you going to buy anything new?*

A: *Yes. We're going to buy a new sofa since this one is ripped. And we're going to add some pictures to make the room look more interesting.*

B: *Great. Are you going to remove anything?*

A: *Yes, we're going to remove one of the chairs to make the room less crowded.*

C. Work with your first partner again. You can change one more thing in the room. What will you change now?

LESSON OBJECTIVES
▸ Understanding and comparing abilities
▸ Understanding descriptions of jobs
▸ Expressing agreement

Lesson 1   Are you interested in sales work?

1 BEFORE YOU LISTEN

Which of these summer jobs look interesting to you? Check (✓) them in the list. Then compare your answers with a partner.

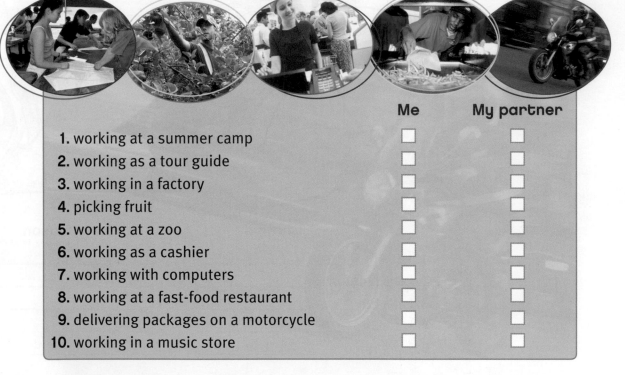

	Me	My partner
1. working at a summer camp	☐	☐
2. working as a tour guide	☐	☐
3. working in a factory	☐	☐
4. picking fruit	☐	☐
5. working at a zoo	☐	☐
6. working as a cashier	☐	☐
7. working with computers	☐	☐
8. working at a fast-food restaurant	☐	☐
9. delivering packages on a motorcycle	☐	☐
10. working in a music store	☐	☐

2 LISTEN AND UNDERSTAND 🎧 CD 3 Track 26

A. Ryan and Anne are looking for summer jobs. Listen and check (✓) the things they can do. Make an X for the things they cannot do. The first one is done for you.

	Ryan	Anne
1. speak Japanese	☑	☒
2. swim	☐	☐
3. draw	☐	☐
4. ride a motorcycle	☐	☐

Anne and Ryan

B. Listen again. Are these statements true or false? Write *T* (true) or *F* (false).

1. The applicant must be at least 21 for this job. ___

2. This job is at a college. ___

3. The applicant needs teaching experience for this job. ___

4. Anne took motorcycle driving classes last spring. ___

3 LISTEN AND UNDERSTAND CD 3 Track 27

A. College students are talking about their jobs last summer. Listen and check (✓) the correct statement.

1. **a.** Julie worked in a factory. ___
   b. Julie did not like the people she worked with. ___

2. **a.** Riko worked with the elephants. ___
   b. Riko played with some of the monkeys. ___

3. **a.** Michael worked on a fruit farm. ___
   b. Michael did not get to travel. ___

4. **a.** Jun-nan made quite a lot of money. ___
   b. Jun-nan did not like the food. ___

B. Listen again. Circle the best ending for each story.

1. **a.** But I made a lot of money.
   b. But I didn't have to work on the weekends.

2. **a.** Luckily, it wasn't my fault.
   b. Luckily, the monkey got lost.

3. **a.** So overall, it was a great experience.
   b. So overall, I'm sorry I went.

4. **a.** So unfortunately, the food was terrible.
   b. So now I'm on a diet.

4 TUNE IN CD 3 Tracks 28 & 29

A. Listen and notice how people express agreement with affirmative and negative statements.

Affirmative statements		Negative statements	
A: *I'd love to work at a summer camp.*	B: *So would I.*	A: *I can't swim.*	B: *Neither can I.*
	B: *I would, too.*		B: *I can't, either.*
	B: *Me, too.*		B: *Me, neither.*
A: *I got a summer job.*	B: *So did I.*	A: *I didn't have much free time.*	B: *Neither did I.*
	B: *I did, too.*		B: *I didn't, either.*
	B: *Me, too.*		B: *Me, neither.*

B. Now listen to short conversations and circle the response you hear.

1. **a.** So do I.   **b.** Neither do I.
2. **a.** So am I.   **b.** Neither am I.
3. **a.** I don't, either.   **b.** I do, too.
4. **a.** I don't, either.   **b.** I do, too.
5. **a.** So am I.   **b.** Neither am I.
6. **a.** Me, neither.   **b.** Me, too.

⑤ AFTER YOU LISTEN

A. What job would be good for you? Complete this survey for yourself. Circle the best number for you.

Find a perfect job for you!

1. Are you good at . . .	very good				very poor
communicating with people?	5	4	3	2	1
helping with people's problems?	5	4	3	2	1
getting work done on time?	5	4	3	2	1
writing stories?	5	4	3	2	1
math?	5	4	3	2	1

2. Can you . . .	very well				not at all
drive a car?	5	4	3	2	1
speak any foreign languages?	5	4	3	2	1
write computer programs?	5	4	3	2	1

3. Are you . . .	very				not at all
friendly?	5	4	3	2	1
practical?	5	4	3	2	1
artistic?	5	4	3	2	1

4. Do you like . . .	very much				not at all
office work?	5	4	3	2	1
working outdoors?	5	4	3	2	1
selling things?	5	4	3	2	1

B. Work with a partner. Take turns asking and answering the questions in the survey. Use these conversations to start but replace the highlighted parts .

A: *Are you good at communicating with people?*　　B: *Can you drive a car?*

B: *Yes, I am. How about you?*　　A: *No, I can't. What about you?*

A: *I am, too.*　　B: *I can't, either.*

A: *Are you friendly ?*　　B: *Do you like office work ?*

B: *Yes, I'm pretty friendly. What about you?*　　A: *No, I don't. How about you?*

A: *Yes, I am, too.*　　B: *Me, neither.*

C. Work with another partner. Look at each other's survey results and take turns suggesting good jobs for each other. Use this example but replace the highlighted parts with jobs in the box and your own information.

a waiter	a teacher	a tour guide	a fashion designer
a store clerk	a summer camp counselor		

A: *You're good at communicating with people. You're good at math.*
　　You're friendly . You don't like office work . I think you would be a good teacher.

LESSON OBJECTIVES
‣ Understanding descriptions of job routines
‣ Recognizing descriptions of occupations
‣ Giving supporting and contrasting information

Lesson 2 What's the job like?

 BEFORE YOU LISTEN

Match each job with its description. Then compare your answers with a partner.

1. a flight attendant ___
2. a fashion model ___
3. a real estate agent ___
4. a doctor ___
5. a camp counselor ___
6. a dance instructor ___
7. a Web site designer ___
8. a veterinarian ___

a. Someone who helps people feel better.
b. Someone who works with animals.
c. Someone who works with children.
d. Someone who wears interesting clothes.
e. Someone who travels a lot.
f. Someone who visits many people's homes.
g. Someone who has to be fit.
h. Someone who works with computers.

2 **LISTEN AND UNDERSTAND** 🎧 CD 3 Track 30

A. People are at a party talking about their jobs. What do they do? Listen and ⟨circle⟩ the correct answer.

1. **a.** Shawn prepares meals.   **b.** Shawn delivers meals.
2. **a.** Yu-ting buys properties.   **b.** Yu-ting shows properties to people.
3. **a.** Yuji sells cars.   **b.** Yuji teaches people how to drive.
4. **a.** Linda prepares food for parties. **b.** Linda has a cooking show on TV.

B. Listen again. Are these statements true or false? Write *T* (true) or *F* (false).

1. Shawn's job is very relaxing. ___
2. Yu-ting advertises properties on the Internet. ___
3. Yuji prepares people for their driving tests. ___
4. Linda gets most weekends off. ___

3 LISTEN AND UNDERSTAND CD 3 Track 31

A. Friends are talking about what they do at work. What are their jobs? Listen and check (✓) the correct answer.

1. **a.** a ski instructor ___   **b.** a dance instructor ___
2. **a.** a chef ___   **b.** a photographer ___
3. **a.** a driving examiner ___   **b.** a police officer ___
4. **a.** a hotel manager ___   **b.** a flight attendant ___

B. Listen again. Check (✓) the correct statement.

Maria

Will

1. **a.** It is a new job. ___
   b. Most of Maria's students are older couples. ___
2. **a.** Tony learned his skills in college. ___
   b. Tony sometimes works outdoors. ___
3. **a.** Will thinks it is an easy job. ___
   b. Sometimes the people have accidents. ___
4. **a.** Sun-young gets very tired. ___
   b. The passengers never complain. ___

Tony

Sun-young

4 TUNE IN 🎧 CD 3 Tracks 32 & 33

A. Listen and notice how people give supporting and contrasting information about an idea.

Supporting information	Contrasting information
It's a lot of fun.	*It's a good business.*
And on top of that, it's good exercise.	*But unfortunately, I have to work every weekend.*
Plus, it's good exercise.	*But the problem is I have to work every weekend.*
What's more, it's good exercise.	*However, I have to work every weekend.*

B. Now listen to other people. Does each person give supporting information or contrasting information? Check (✓) the correct column.

	Supporting information	Contrasting information
1.	☐	☐
2.	☐	☐
3.	☐	☐
4.	☐	☐
5.	☐	☐
6.	☐	☐

AFTER YOU LISTEN

A. What do you think about these jobs? Individually, choose words in the box to describe each job. Then compare your answers with a partner using this conversation but replace the highlighted parts with different jobs and the words in the box.

relaxing	exciting	difficult	dangerous
boring	well paid	poorly paid	fun
interesting	nerve-racking	stressful	rewarding

1. a ski instructor _____

2. a doctor _____

3. an actor _____

4. a dance teacher _____

5. a magician's assistant _____

6. a science teacher _____

7. a fashion model _____

8. a truck driver _____

9. a rock singer _____

A: *What do you think about being a ski instructor?*

B: *I think being a ski instructor is fun. However, it's quite dangerous.*

A: *What do you think about being a doctor?*

B: *I think being a doctor is very difficult. What's more, it's quite stressful.*

B. Work with your partner. What other jobs have these qualities? Write them in the list.

1. stressful and nerve-racking _____

2. exciting but dangerous _____

3. interesting and rewarding _____

4. well paid but boring _____

5. poorly paid but rewarding _____

Talents & Abilities

LESSON OBJECTIVES
› Understanding descriptions of abilities
› Recognizing items from descriptions
› Answering questions

Lesson 1   Can you dance the tango?

1 **BEFORE YOU LISTEN**

Which of these activities can you do? Check (✓) them in the list. Add two other activities you can do. Then ask a partner and compare your answers.

	Me	My partner
1. play the piano	☐	☐
2. speak Japanese	☐	☐
3. stand on your head	☐	☐
4. make pizza	☐	☐
5. read music	☐	☐
6. write a computer program	☐	☐
7. dance the tango	☐	☐
8. play chess	☐	☐
9. type fast	☐	☐
10. ice-skate	☐	☐
11. _____	☐	☐
12. _____	☐	☐

2 **LISTEN AND UNDERSTAND** 🎧 CD 3 Track 34

A. Eun-joo and Paul are talking about things they can do. Listen and number these activities from 1 to 4.

a. play the piano ___   **b.** cook ___   **c.** speak Japanese ___   **d.** type on a computer ___

B. Listen again. Who is better at each activity: Eun-joo or Paul? Circle the correct answer.

1. **a.** Eun-joo   **b.** Paul
2. **a.** Eun-joo   **b.** Paul
3. **a.** Eun-joo   **b.** Paul
4. **a.** Eun-joo   **b.** Paul

LISTEN AND UNDERSTAND CD 3 Track 35

A. Parents are talking with department store clerks about gifts for their children. Listen and number these items from 1 to 5.

a. an electronic dictionary ____   **b.** a video camera ____   **c.** ice skates ____

d. a keyboard ____   **e.** snorkeling equipment ____

B. Listen again. Are these statements true or false? Write *T* (true) or *F* (false).

1. Her son is a weak swimmer. ____
2. His daughter has had a lot of lessons. ____
3. His son joined a film club in college. ____
4. It contains about 5,000 words. ____
5. The father is an excellent skater. ____

4 **TUNE IN** CD 3 Tracks 36 & 37

A. Listen and notice how people answer questions and give additional information.

> **A:** *Did you find it difficult to learn Japanese?*
> **B:** *Yes, I did.* **But going to Japan for a summer really helped.**
>
> **A:** *Is he a good swimmer?*
> **B:** *Oh, yes, he is.* **He's on the school team.**

B. Now match each question with its answer. Then listen and check your answers.

1. Can you play chess? ____
2. Do you know how to design a Web site? ____
3. Can you do tai chi? ____
4. Are you good at fixing things? ____
5. Can you dance the tango? ____

a. No, I'm not. I always get other people to fix them.
b. No, I can't. But I hear it's a good way to keep fit.
c. Yes, I do. I've designed quite a few.
d. No, I can't. But I've always wanted to learn how to play it.
e. No, I can't. I love music, but I'm a terrible dancer!

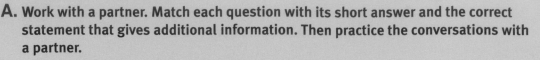

5 AFTER YOU LISTEN

A. Work with a partner. Match each question with its short answer and the correct statement that gives additional information. Then practice the conversations with a partner.

1. Can you play a musical instrument? ___
2. Do you know how to cook? ___
3. Can you dance the tango? ___
4. Can you ice-skate? ___
5. Can you ride a motorcycle? ___

a. No, I can't. I'd like to get one, but my parents say they're too dangerous.
b. Yes, a little. But I prefer in-line skating.
c. Yeah! I love it, and now I'm taking salsa lessons.
d. Yes, I can. I play the violin. I'm in the school orchestra.
e. Not very well. But I'm getting better. My roommate's helping me.

B. Individually, write your own answers to the questions in part A and add more information. Then work with a partner. Take turns asking and answering the questions and write your partner's answers. Use these conversations but replace the highlighted parts with your own information.

Me	My partner
1. _____	_____
2. _____	_____
3. _____	_____
4. _____	_____
5. _____	_____

A: *Can you play a musical instrument?*
B: *Yes, I can. I play the flute. Can you play a musical instrument?*
A: *No, I can't. I wish I could play the guitar.*

B: *Do you know how to cook?*
A: *Not really. But I make great sandwiches. Do you?*
B: *Yes, I do. I cook most of our meals at home.*

C. Think of two more questions to ask your partner. Take turns asking and answering the questions. Use the conversations in part B.

1. Can you _____?
2. Do you know how to _____?

LESSON OBJECTIVES
▸ Recognizing descriptions of talents
▸ Understanding information about people
▸ Keeping conversations going

Lesson 2 What are you good at?

1 BEFORE YOU LISTEN

A. Match each talent with its description. Then compare your answers with a partner.

1. linguistic ___
2. mathematical ___
3. musical ___
4. naturalist ___
5. artistic ___
6. interpersonal ___
7. self-reflective ___
8. physical ___

a. good at logical and scientific thinking and problem-solving
b. good at languages, reading, writing, and storytelling
c. good at using your hands and body, sports, and dance
d. good at painting, decorating, and photography
e. good at singing, creating rhythms, and playing instruments
f. good at understanding yourself and your feelings
g. good at understanding and working with other people
h. good at recognizing and classifying plants and animals

B. What are your talents? Circle your three best talents in part A. Then compare your answers with a partner.

2 LISTEN AND UNDERSTAND 🎧 CD 3 Track 38

A. People are talking about activities they are good at. Listen and circle the talent they describe.

1. **a.** naturalist	**b.** interpersonal	**c.** physical
2. **a.** artistic	**b.** linguistic	**c.** musical
3. **a.** linguistic	**b.** interpersonal	**c.** mathematical

B. Listen again. What will each person say next? Check (✓) the best follow-up question.

1. **a.** So what kind of phone do you have? ___
   b. So do you like giving advice? ___

2. **a.** And what colors do you like the best? ___
   b. And where do you live? ___

3. **a.** Hmm. Are you planning to go there? ___
   b. Hmm. Is that what you want to do? ___

3 LISTEN AND UNDERSTAND 🎧 CD 3 Track 39

A. A TV talk show host is talking to young people about their abilities. Are these statements true or false? Write *T* (true) or *F* (false).

1. Hyun-joo has not sold any paintings yet. ___
2. Koichi did not have a good voice when he was five. ___
3. Allison started playing tennis when she was a teenager. ___
4. Patrick's parents speak many languages. ___

Hyun-joo

Allison

B. Listen again. What do you think the host will say next? Check (✓) the best answer.

1. **a.** That's too bad. ___
   b. That's wonderful. ___

2. **a.** That must be really delicious. ___
   b. That must be very exciting. ___

3. **a.** Your parents must be very proud of you. ___
   b. You should get a new racket. ___

4. **a.** You should try to learn more languages. ___
   b. You could get a job as a translator. ___

Koichi

Patrick

4 TUNE IN 🎧 CD 3 Tracks 40 & 41

A. Listen and notice how people keep conversations going by repeating information and asking follow-up questions.

> **A:** *I usually paint the walls every year.*
> **B:** *Every year! Wow. Is that necessary?*
>
> **A:** *I'm a freshman in the school of engineering.*
> **B:** *Engineering! That's interesting. Why did you choose engineering?*
>
> **A:** *I'm learning two more languages at the moment.*
> **B:** *Two more! Which ones?*

B. Now circle the key words in each sentence that you think the second person will repeat. Then listen and check your answers.

1. I won a sports prize at school last year.
2. When I went to college, I was the youngest person in my class.
3. I've always liked animals, and we had a lot of pets when I was a child.
4. After I graduated from college, I got a small part in a TV show.
5. I got interested in dance after I saw a famous Russian ballet dancer perform.

5 AFTER YOU LISTEN

A. What do you like to do? Complete this survey for yourself. Check (✓) the statements that are true for you in the list.

¡Tenga un buen viaje!

	Me	My partner
1. I enjoy music and I play two instruments.	☐	☐
2. I love the outdoors and I enjoy hiking.	☐	☐
3. I spend all of my free time on a hobby.	☐	☐
4. I enjoy learning new languages.	☐	☐
5. I love animals and I have a pet.	☐	☐
6. I have a good sense of design, and people say I am artistic.	☐	☐
7. I enjoy making things and working with my hands.	☐	☐
8. I love food and I enjoy cooking.	☐	☐
9. I am very healthy and I exercise a lot.	☐	☐
10. I love math and I enjoy solving problems.	☐	☐

B. Work with a partner. Take turns asking and answering questions about the statements that are true for you. Complete the survey for your partner. Use these conversations to start but replace the highlighted parts with your own information.

A: *I enjoy music and I play two musical instruments.*

B: *Two instruments! That's amazing. Which ones do you play?*

A: *Well, I play the piano and the saxophone.*

B: *I enjoy making things and working with my hands.*

A: *Making things! That sounds interesting. What do you make?*

B: *I make bird houses and other things out of wood.*

Student CD Track List

This CD contains the final **Listen and Understand** of each lesson.

Track	Unit	Content
01		Title and copyright
02 & 03	Unit 1	Lesson 1, *page 3*
04		Lesson 2, *page 6*
05	Unit 2	Lesson 1, *page 9*
06		Lesson 2, *page 12*
07	Unit 3	Lesson 1, *page 15*
08		Lesson 2, *page 18*
09	Unit 4	Lesson 1, *page 21*
10		Lesson 2, *page 24*
11	Unit 5	Lesson 1, *page 27*
12		Lesson 2, *page 30*
13	Unit 6	Lesson 1, *page 33*
14		Lesson 2, *page 36*
15	Unit 7	Lesson 1, *page 39*
16		Lesson 2, *page 42*
17	Unit 8	Lesson 1, *page 45*
18		Lesson 2, *page 48*
19	Unit 9	Lesson 1, *page 51*
20		Lesson 2, *page 54*
21	Unit 10	Lesson 1, *page 57*
22		Lesson 2, *page 60*
23	Unit 11	Lesson 1, *page 63*
24		Lesson 2, *page 66*
25	Unit 12	Lesson 1, *page 69*
26		Lesson 2, *page 72*
27	Unit 13	Lesson 1, *page 75*
28		Lesson 2, *page 78*
29	Unit 14	Lesson 1, *page 81*
30		Lesson 2, *page 84*
31	Unit 15	Lesson 1, *page 87*
32		Lesson 2, *page 90*